P9-DDZ-974

# Christianity
# in
# Modern Korea

Lincoln Christian College

*The Asia Society* is a nonprofit, nonpartisan public education organization dedicated to increasing American understanding of Asia and its growing importance to the United States and to world relations. Founded in 1956, the Society covers all of Asia—22 countries from Japan to Iran and from Soviet Central Asia to the South Pacific islands. Through its programs in contemporary affairs, the fine and performing arts, and elementary and secondary education, the Society reaches audiences across the United States and works closely with colleagues in Asia.

The *Asian Agenda* program of The Asia Society seeks to . . .

- Alert Americans to the key Asian issues of the 1980s
- Illuminate the policy choices facing decision-makers in the public and private sectors
- Strengthen the dialogue between Americans and Asians on the issues and their policy implications.

*Asian Agenda* issues are identified in consultation with a group of advisors and are addressed through studies and publications, national and international conferences, public programs around the U.S., and media activities. Major funding for the Asian Agenda program is currently provided by the Ford Foundation, the Rockefeller Foundation, the Andrew W. Mellon Foundation, the Henry Luce Foundation, the Rockefeller Brothers Fund, and the United States-Japan Foundation.

Responsibility for the facts and opinions expressed in this publication rests exclusively with the author. His opinions and interpretations do not necessarily reflect the views of The Asia Society or its supporters.

# Christianity
# in
# Modern Korea

## Donald N. Clark

UNIVERSITY
PRESS OF
AMERICA

LANHAM • NEW YORK • LONDON

THE
ASIA
SOCIETY

Copyright © 1986 by

University Press of America,® Inc.

4720 Boston Way
Lanham, MD 20706

3 Henrietta Street
London WC2E 8LU England

All rights reserved

Printed in the United States of America

Co-published by arrangement with
The Asia Society,
725 Park Avenue, New York, New York 10021

**Library of Congress Cataloging in Publication Data**

Clark, Donald N.
  Christianity in modern Korea.

  (Asian agenda report ; 5)
  Bibliography: p.
  1. Korea (South)—Church history.   2. Korea—Church
history.   I. Title.   II. Series.
BR1328.C53    1986       275.19'5       86-9092
ISBN 0-8191-5384-2 (alk. paper)
ISBN 0-8191-5385-0 (pbk. : alk. paper)

All University Press of America books are produced on acid-free
paper which exceeds the minimum standards set by the National
Historical Publications and Records Commission.

# CONTENTS

# FOREWORD

Over the centuries religion has had a varied but profound influence on the shape of Asian societies and the course of Asian events. During the twentieth century religion has sometimes been an important component of nationalism, and religious organizations played roles in independence movements in many Asian countries. Following independence, however, many Asian governments sought to control these forces, viewing them as threatening to fragile national unity and contrary to the secularism believed to be necessary for modernization. Today religion is again emerging as a powerful determinant of national affairs in many Asian countries.

It comes as a surprise to many Americans that Christianity is a significant and often controversial presence in Asia. An estimated 104 million Christians, about 10% of the global total, live in non-Oceanic Asia. Although there are Christians in virtually every Asian society, they are most heavily concentrated in two countries, the Philippines and South Korea. In both Korean and Philippine history Christianity has been a powerful social and political force, and today the churches are deeply involved in the most pressing issues facing South Korea and the Philippines.

This Asian Agenda report on Christianity in modern Korea by Donald N. Clark is part of a larger effort by The Asia Society to explore for a wide American audience the impact of religion and culture on public life in contemporary Asia. In 1984 the Society sponsored an international conference and a series of public programs across the United States on "Islam and Public Life in Asia". Under the editorship of project director Dr. John Esposito of Holy Cross College, the conference papers will be published in a volume by Oxford University Press in mid-1986. One of those papers, "International Relations of the Asian Muslim States," by Dr. James Piscatori, is also being published separately in March 1986. For future reports on religion and public life in Asia, the Society plans to examine Christianity in the Philippines, Hindusism in India and Budhism in Thailand.

*Christianity in Modern Korea* is the fifth in a new series of reports produced by The Asia Society's national public education program on contemporary Asian affairs, "America's Asian Agenda." The Asian Agenda program seeks to alert Americans to critical issues in Asian affairs and in U.S.-Asian relations, to illuminate the choices which public and private policymakers face and to strengthen trans-Pacific dialogue on the issues. Through studies, national and international conferences, regional public programs in the United States, and corporate and media activities, the program involved American and Asian specialists and opinion leaders in a far-reaching educational process. Asian Agenda publications emphasize short, timely reports aimed at a wide readership. Other Asian Agenda reports to be published in 1986 will address a variety of topics including the Philippines and U.S.-Philippine relations, the United States and the ANZUS alliance, Japan, the United States and a changing Northeast Asia, and financing Asian growth and development.

The Asia Society is indebted to a number of individuals and organizations for their roles in making this report possible. First and foremost we would like to thank Donald N. Clark for the intelligence, understanding, patience and openness he has brought to this task. The Society is fortunate to have found a scholar so deeply knowledgeable about Korea and willing to commit himself to our public education objectives. We are grateful to a number of other individuals who assisted in the development of the manuscript, including William Gleysteen, Han Sung-joo, Laurel Kendall, Chong-Sik Lee, and Donald MacDonald. As always, various members of the Society's Asian Agenda Advisory Group, co-chaired by David D. Newsom and Robert A. Scalapino, provided valuable guidance.

Financial support for this project came from several sources. We are grateful to the Andrew W. Mellon Foundation for funding of this and other Society projects that bring humanistic perspectives to bear on contemporary issues. General support for the Asian Agenda program has been generously provided by the Ford, Rockefeller, and Henry Luce foundations and the Rockefeller Brothers Fund.

Several members of The Asia Society's staff were involved in the development of this publication. David G. Timberman deserves the greatest credit for his central role in identifying the topic and author and in working with Professor Clark to ensure the best manuscript. Eileen D. Chang and Sara E. Robertson brought the manuscript to press. Emily Collins provided essential administrative support throughout the process.


Marshall M. Bouton
Director, Public Affairs
12 February 1986

# ACKNOWLEDGMENTS

This report is based on research conducted in Seoul in 1983–84 under a grant from the Korean-American Educational [Fulbright] Commission while on leave from my faculty position at Trinity University in San Antonio. I am also grateful to Yonsei University in Seoul for providing me with a base from which to study American-Korean relations and the history of Korean Christianity. In Seoul I learned much from Horace G. Underwood and from Profs. Min Kyongbae, Yi Manyol, Lew Young-ick, and David Kwang-sun Suh, among many others, and from L. George Paik, President-Emeritus of Yonsei, who shared many hours of conversation with me in the year just prior to his death at the age of 90. Without the help of these benefactors and teachers, this report could not have been written. The opinions and conclusions expressed in this work, of course, are my own.

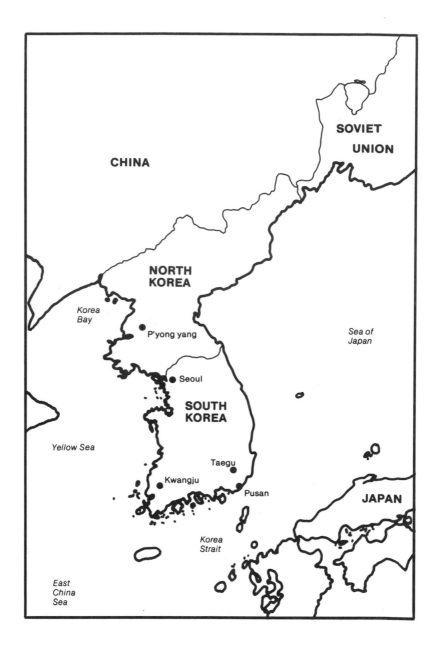

CHINA

SOVIET
UNION

NORTH
KOREA

Korea
Bay

● P'yong yang

Sea of
Japan

● Seoul

SOUTH
KOREA

Yellow Sea

Taegu ●

Kwangju ●

● Pusan

JAPAN

Korea
Strait

East
China
Sea

# Executive Summary

Christianity has enjoyed unique success in Korea. Since the introduction of Catholic worship in 1784 and the coming of Protestant missionaries in 1884, Christianity has become Korea's second largest religion, after Buddhism, with over nine million members in a variety of denominations. The influence of the church is apparent everywhere in Korea today.

The first Korean Christians could not have foreseen such spectacular growth. Prior to the 1880s the Confucianist Korean government outlawed Christianity, carrying on persecutions which cost the lives of thousands of early believers. After Korea's opening to the West in 1882, however, the Korean imperial court gave in to Western pressure and admitted foreign missionaries.

The Protestant workers who came to Korea from the West around the turn of the century set up churches, schools and hospitals. Schools were especially welcome in Korea among common people who had never been able to acquire education before. The missionaries' use of the simple Korean *Han'gŭl* alphabet contributed to the spread of literacy. Churches also developed rapidly, particularly in the northwest around the city of Pyongyang.

When Japan annexed Korea in 1910, the Christian community put up resistance. With Japanese gendarmes enforcing obedience throughout the Korean Peninsula, the church was one of the few places where Koreans could express themselves. Despite Japanese pressure the church grew rapidly. In fact, one unique feature of Christianity in Korea is that it sided with the people against a colonial power, whereas elsewhere it was often seen as part of the imperialist presence.

The Allied occupation and division of Korea in 1945 led to a mass exodus of Christians from the Soviet-occupied North to the American-occupied South. The new church was virtually independent of missionaries but the legacy of Japanese rule and the upheavals of national division caused serious conflicts. These were aggravated by the Korean War, 1950–53, in which the church suffered heavily and lost much of its leadership. After 1953 new denominations split off as the Christian community suffered extreme factionalism. Social and economic conditions after the war bred a spiritual crisis in Korea that was reflected in conflicts within the church.

The 1960s saw several major trends develop in the Korean church. One was a spectacular growth rate. Another was the complete devolution of control of church institutions from foreign to Korean hands. Yet another was a new evangelical fervor, demonstrated in great crusade meetings. New seminaries and training programs helped offset the losses of the Korean War. Women, who make up three-quarters of the church membership, began to take on a more assertive role. The National Council of Churches pooled the resources of the Protestant denominations to create unified ministries in broadcasting, publishing and social welfare.

Korean Christianity today, both Protestant and Catholic, is basically conservative, concerned with maintaining social and political stability and enjoying the improving living standards of the past 30 years. While critics of the church may accuse it of complacency, most Christian institutions stay quiet politically and stress the spiritual needs of their followers.

Korea has many exemplary churches, including the Yŏngnak Presbyterian Church and the Central Full Gospel (Pentecostal) Church both in Seoul. Yŏngnak began in North Korea but its congregation and minister fled south after World War II and set up the church anew in Seoul, serving refugees. Despite formidable obstacles it has become a major complex, with thousands of members and programs to meet many kinds of social and spiritual needs. Bigger still is the newer Central Full Gospel church, with 325,000 members and an enormous establishment with ministries and study cells all over the city. Both churches are evidence of the attraction of Christianity in modern Korean life and of the community service the church performs amid the disorder and alienation of modern urban life.

Church outreach in Korea takes many forms. Christian universities are among Korea's best. Church-sponsored hospitals and clinics have consistently led the way in health care delivery for the Korean people. Among the many special programs are those which assist workers in factories, children in need of adoption and girls from the countryside in search of city jobs. The churches sponsor extensive ministries to students on campuses, and to soldiers through the chaplaincy. Christian radio stations carry the message into every corner of Korea— including the North. Church organizations supply Gideon Bibles for hotels and Christian programs on videotape to entertain passengers on intercity buses. Foreign Christians are invited to Korea to study the methods of church expansion in special institutes, and young Koreans are encouraged to volunteer for missionary service abroad.

The Catholic church, though a quarter the size of the combined Protestant church, has experienced proportional growth since the Korean War. Largely dependent on a foreign priesthood prior to 1940, the postwar years have seen a steady increase in Korean leadership and elaboration of types of institutions. A high point for Korean Catholics was the bicentennial mass in 1984, at which Pope John Paul II presided over the canonization of 103 martyrs from Korean church history.

Many analysts have tried to explain the reasons for church growth in Korea when in neighboring countries, notably China and Japan, the number of converts has been so much smaller. Historical conditions in

Korea seem to account for some of it. Another reason may be that Koreans saw Christianity as "modern," but not "imperialist." Another is that the church, for all its faults, has shown a kind of integrity which has been lacking in many other modern Korean institutions.

Controversy has grown among a dissenting minority of the Korean church representing a mixture of sects and denominations that has repeatedly questioned the government's commitment to democracy and human rights. Beginning in the late 1960s, the dissenters confronted the government over labor relations and working conditions, human rights abuses, and government repression of the political opposition. It became common for Christian leaders—ministers, professors, politicians and writers—to go to prison for challenging the total control of President Park Chung Hee in the 1970s. Since the rise of Chun Doo Hwan in 1980, much of the Christian opposition has been cowed or coopted into silence. Yet a significant number of Christian leaders have managed to keep up a public witness, tying political freedom to religious toleration.

Christianity is inextricably linked to American-Korean relations by virtue of the fact that so many American missionaries have worked in Korea and that the Korean church is so closely oriented to the West, especially the United States. In a sense, the evolution of the Korean church from a client, or creation, of foreign missionaries was a process akin to what is now happening in American-Korean relations, as South Korea becomes a partner and competitor economically, and its leaders rely less and less on foreign advice and assistance.

The Korean church today seems fairly content with current trends. It does not seem likely to develop into a coherent political force in the future, though it would be formidable if events were to politicize so large a membership. Rather, Christians will continue, both individually and collectively, to lead Korea's modernization and to be a force for restraint and humane values in a society undergoing rapid change.

# I. Introduction: Christianity in Contemporary Korea

There is no mistaking the omnipresence of Christianity in Korea today. It shows in the steeples that crown the hilltops and the neon crosses that light up everywhere at night on chapels and storefront churches. It shows in apartment buildings, where believers display plaques on their doors proclaiming membership in such-and-such a church. The statistics are impressive. In 1981 there were 2,353 Catholic and 23,346 Protestant congregations, with a total membership of 9,076,788 out of a total population of roughly 40 million, or 25 percent. Christianity was a close second to Buddhism and gaining, and far ahead of Ch'ŏndogyo, the Korean "Religion of the Heavenly Way," which was third with 1.2 million members.[1]

Christianity is conspicuous in other ways: in the bells that peal forth at four o'clock in the morning calling the faithful to prayer and the loud-speakers that broadcast hymns across the rooftops at all hours; in the next-door church that holds all-night prayer festivals with singing and chanting; in the Christian icons on bus and taxi dashboards; in the gospel newspapers distributed on street corners and in subway stations; in predictable places such as the Salvation Army's Christmas collections and in unpredictable places such as the "Christian Bakery," or the "Christian Optometrist," whose eye chart is made up of Bible verses in letters of diminishing size.

Christianity in Korea is not only highly visible, it is aggressive and dynamic. The Full Gospel (Pentacostal) Church on Yŏido Island in the Han River has a membership of over 325,000, a pastoral staff of over a hundred, multiple services each Sunday, a domestic radio and television ministry and a regular religious telecast for the Korean community of Los Angeles. It is already the world's largest church, and growing fast. In Yŏido Plaza, Seoul's square for mass rallies, Christian crusades frequently muster crowds of over a million. The churches send missionaries to such countries as Thailand, Brazil, the Philippines, India and Pakistan, and support Korean congregations in America. There is a Korean Y.M.C.A., Y.W.C.A., Bible Society, Christian Literature Society, two Christian broadcasting organizations and a large number of Christian schools, colleges and universities.

Christianity in Korea is also controversial. Disputes over theology have led to the proliferation of denominations and sects—and even a few new heterodoxies such as the Unification Church of the Reverend Sun Myung Moon and the Olive Tree Cult of Elder Pak T'ae-sŏn. Class and regional rivalries have further fragmented the church, as have

[1]James H. Grayson and Ruth H. Grayson, editors, *Prayer Calendar of Christian Missions in Korea and General Directory*, Seoul: Christian Literature Society, 1983, p. 219.

political crises under Japanese colonial rule (1910–1945) and the cold war era, during which Korea has been divided into North and South. The early missionaries may have been somewhat responsible: there have been four separate Presbyterian missions from the United States alone over the years, and one each from Australia and Canada. Although they cooperated and tried to create a unified Korean Presbyterian church, there are now four major Presbyterian denominations in Korea:

> *Presbyterian Church of Korea (ecumenical), 4,100 churches*
> *Presbyterian Church of Korea (non-ecumenical), 5,062*
>   *churches*
> *Presbyterian Church in the Republic of Korea, 892 churches;*
> *Presbyterian Church of Korea (Koryŏ Seminary Faction),*
>   *703 churches[2]*

Other Protestant denominations suffer similar fractious tendencies, but they are not so conspicuous since their memberships are not as large. Presbyterians are the largest Christian denomination, with more than three million members. Roman Catholics number 1.6 million. Other denominations include Methodist, Holiness, Baptist, Pentecostal, Church of Christ, Seventh Day Adventist, Salvation Army, Nazarene, Anglican and Lutheran. The Mormons began a major missionary effort in Korea in the mid-1960s and have made some converts. There is even one lone Quaker church with a membership of 20. Most denominations have seminaries to train their clergy; many have schools and colleges. Most also support good works such as orphanages, old people's homes, and schools for the handicapped. There are still missionaries from abroad, but with few exceptions they work within the hierarchies of the Korean church and are diminishing in number. Christianity, it may truly be said, is now a Korean religion.

1984 saw the bicentennial of Catholicism and the centennial of Protestantism in Korea. Both anniversaries were greeted with great ceremony. In May, Pope John Paul II celebrated a special mass in Yŏido Plaza in which 103 martyrs of the Korean church were canonized. In August, the Protestant centenary celebration drew an estimated 3.5 million believers to a series of rallies to hear sermons by various Christian leaders, including Dr. Billy Graham. Other observances continue to take place as church-related institutions mark their centenaries. Yonsei, the foremost Protestant university, marked its hundredth birthday in May 1985.

As the church passes these milestones it is troubled by growing confrontations between conservative/evangelical and liberal/activist wings and between church and state over human rights. Most Korean Chris-

---

[2]G. Thompson Brown, *Not by Might: A Century of Presbyterians in Korea,* Atlanta: General Assembly Mission Board, Presbyterian Church (U.S.), 1984, p. iv.

tians are apolitical or politically conservative, but an articulate minority believe in a Christian duty to struggle for economic and social justice. This group seethes with anger not only against the government, but also against other elements of the church, which accept the repression because the government is anti-communist and because life in South Korea, despite turmoil, is rapidly getting better. The anger, not surprisingly, is a creative engine in Korean Christianity, producing dynamic leaders and a new Korean-style theology. Troublesome though it may seem to the authorities, it is another sign of the vitality of the Christian religion in Korea.

Christianity has experienced remarkable growth in Korea which, like its neighbors China and Japan, is a traditionally Confucian society. Its basic religious tradition is shamanist, but this is overlaid with centuries of Buddhist and Confucianist influence from China. When Christianity collided with similar traditions in China it gained ground very slowly, and although it survived the tribulations of Maoism, its impact on contemporary Chinese society is miniscule. The Japanese church is also small by comparison. Why, then, has the Korean church grown so dramatically? What accounts for its vitality, appeal and intramural strife? What part does the church play in Korean politics? What are the implications of the church's growth and progress for American-Korean relations, and what should Americans know about it?

# II. An Outline of Korean Christianity, 1784–1945

## Catholic Beginnings

The Korean church began with a small group of eighteenth-century Confucian scholars from the out-of-power political faction, *Silhak*, or the School of Practical Learning. The purpose of *Silhak* was a rejuvenation of Korean Confucianism through a clearer understanding of man's relation to nature—"the investigation of things." Among the texts studied by the *Silhak* scholars was a smuggled copy of *The True Doctrine of the Lord of Heaven*, a Chinese work by the seventeeth-century Jesuit missionary Matteo Ricci. Ricci's description of the Christian God seemed much like their idea of the Neo-Confucian Supreme Ultimate, and they decided to learn more. This was risky. The Pope's condemnation of ancestor worship in 1742 had scandalized Korean Confucianists; the church was therefore anathema to the orthodox atmosphere of Yi-dynasty Korea.

High in the mountains of Kyonggi Province, in the Buddhist hermitage of Chŏnjin-am, the Silhak scholar Yi Pyŏk and his friends decided to send a representative to Peking to investigate. They were acquainted with Yi Sŭng-hun, son of a recently-appointed Korean tribute envoy bound for China in 1783, and they persuaded him to accompany the envoy, find out everything he could, and bring back books. Yi Sŭng-hun did more: in Peking he became a Christian himself and was christened Peter, a name suggesting his destiny as founder of the Korean church. When he returned home in 1784, he carried books, crucifixes, images and information about Christian rituals. Then he joined with Yi Pyŏk to found a small lay congregation of Catholics. This was Korea's first-known Christian church.

Soon the church began to grow. Since the leaders were not ordained and could not perform baptisms they sent to Peking for a priest, and were joined in 1794 by a Chinese missionary, James Chou Wen-mu. By that time the government was aware of the spreading heresy and was arresting Christians. Father Chou himself was caught and executed in 1801.

Numerous Korean Christians were put to death as waves of persecution followed. Despite this, the church continued to grow. During the persecution of 1839, French missionaries were among those killed. In the persecution of 1846, the first Korean priest, Andrew Kim Tae-gŏn, was executed less than a year after his return from theological training in Macao. But even the fear of execution did not deter people from joining the church. The contemporary Catholic church on Chŏltu-san—"Head-chopping Hill"—is a moving memorial to the Korean martyrs, and its museum displays the various torture instruments used to force them to recant.

Thus the church continued to gather adherents, adding women and then children—whole families—as generations passed. Times were hard anyway, and Christians at least had a network of mutual support among commoners who were oppressed by landlords, prefects and moneylenders. In fact, evading the law was a popular pastime, and a religious doctrine that affirmed the value of persons, promised a better afterlife, and provided a certain safety in numbers had its attractions. More missionaries stole into Korea in various disguises and led services in safe houses. Some survived; some were killed. Nine Frenchmen were executed in 1866 in the most terrible persecution of all, along with an estimated 2,000 converts. Arrests went on until the opening of Korea in the early 1880s, by which time it was widely understood that Korea was no safe place for missionary work.

**Protestant Beginnings**

While the Korean Catholic community was suffering in the nine-teenth century, the Protestant faith was also putting down roots. In Chinese Manchuria, in the 1870s Scottish missionaries studied Korean and then translated scriptures, which they passed to itinerant Korean merchants. The merchants in turn set up small family congregations in Korea. The first Protestant church was founded in Sŏrae, Hwanghae Province, by a merchant named Sŏ Sang-yun.

Protestant missions to Korea began in 1884 when Dr. Horace N. Allen was transferred from the Presbyterian Mission in China. To gain access to Korea, he came not as a missionary but as physician to the U.S. Lega-tion in Seoul. A short-lived palace coup in December 1884 gave him the chance to heal the wounds of a Korean prince, thereby earning the grat-itude of the king and permission to start a clinic. He also won toleration for religious missionary work in Seoul. In 1885 missionary work began in earnest with Horace G. Underwood and Henry G. Appenzeller, Presbyterian and Methodist, respectively. Underwood's descendants are still active in Korea, in the church and university (Yonsei) which he founded. Appenzeller's children likewise helped build two of Korea's finest schools, Paejae Boys' High School and Ewha Women's University.

**Expansion of Protestant work.** Many other pioneers joined these early workers before the turn of the century. They pushed government toleration to the limit and fanned out across the country, opening little stations in all the provinces. To avoid duplicating their efforts, the vari-ous missions agreed to work in different areas of the country. The most successful work in terms of numbers and church growth was accom-plished in northwest Korea around Pyongyang, the present capital of communist North Korea. This field was assigned to the American Northern Presbyterian Mission.

The missionaries converted more people to the Protestant faith in

Pyongyang region than in other parts of Korea. This area was located in a corridor between Seoul and the Chinese border, and thus was somewhat accustomed to foreign influence. The farms were not as productive as those in the more fertile south, and there were fewer of the land-based aristocracy, who tended to be conservative, Confucian and anti-Christian. Many commoners in this area lacked land and made their living by their wits; in the south they were considered scrappy and uncouth. It was a noteworthy development, therefore, when the missionaries came on the scene professing a religion which was meant for even the coarsest person. In the eyes of Koreans, it was even more remarkable when they founded schools and opened them to commoners' children. The traditional educational system seemed to have been set up to exclude from advancement all but the highest-born. Here was opportunity knocking, and the church made impressive gains.

For many years Pyongyang thrived as a Christian center. Around the turn of the century it began to develop as a regional hub for the Northern Presbyterian Mission (U.S.A.) and as an urban center for the Methodists, who had joined the Presbyterians in medical and educational work there. Catholics also set up a station in Pyongyang, creating a diocesan headquarters under The Catholic Foreign Mission Society of America (Maryknolls) in 1927. All Christians working in the area felt a certain pride in the progress of the church, but it was the Northern Presbyterians who invested most heavily in Pyongyang, and it was their denomination which developed the greatest momentum in the area. There was a special esprit de corps among the Pyongyang Presbyterians. They touted their compound as the largest mission station in the world and even had a map printed up on the back of their business stationery to illustrate the scale of their work. By the late 1920s they were operating a college (Sungsil, or "Union Christian College"), a church, a seminary, a girls' academy, Bible institutes for men and women, a hospital (the Union Christian Hospital), and a boarding school for missionary children. Because of this massive effort, Pyongyang outshone all other mission stations in Korea in the number of converts, and it was through their efforts in Pyongyang that the Presbyterian denomination developed its long-standing numerical advantage over other Christian churches in the country.

**The Great Revival of 1907.** The tone for Korean Protestantism was actually set in 1907, at a series of revival meetings in Pyongyang. That year was one of great despair in Korea. Living conditions were bad, the Russo-Japanese War had just ended with Japan's winning a free hand in Korea, the Japanese had reduced Korea to a protectorate, and it seemed that independence was about to be lost. The Pyongyang revival of 1907 was a mass meeting in which churchmembers by the thousands became caught up in an emotional wave that swept over the entire Korean church. An eyewitness account suggests the flavor of the event:

7

> After a short sermon Dr. [Graham] Lee took charge of the meeting and called for prayers. So many began praying that Dr. Lee said, 'If you want to pray like that, all pray,' and the whole audience began to pray out loud, all together. The effect was indescribable. Not confusion, but a vast harmony of sound and spirit, a mingling together of souls moved by an irresistible impulse to prayer. It sounded to me like the falling of many waters, an ocean of prayer beating against God's throne . . . .
>
> As the prayer continued, a spirit of heaviness and sorrow came upon the audience. Over on one side, someone began to weep and, in a moment, the whole congregation was weeping . . . .
>
> Man after man would rise, confess his sin, break down and weep, and then throw himself to the floor and beat the floor with his fists in a perfect agony of conviction . . . . Sometimes after a confession, the whole audience would break out in audible prayer and the effect . . . was something indescribable . . . . And so the meeting went on until two o'clock a.m., with confession and weeping and praying.[3]

L. George Paik, the great Christian educator, looked back on the Pyongyang revival as a Great Awakening: "The religious experience of the people gave to the Christian church in Korea a character which is its own . . . . Korean Christians of today look back on the movement as the source of their spiritual life."[4]

Foreign missionaries may take credit for much of what was started in Korean Christianity. Their work took on three main forms: church-founding, medical work and education. Church-founding and the training of a native pastorate were their primary concern, but medicine and education were vital to the modernization of Korea. Mission schools were the only modern schools prior to World War I, and although there was some question about the curriculum—whether it should be the Bible alone, or include modern, "secular" subjects as well—a large number of Korea's postwar leaders had spent some time in mission schools.

### Christianity and Nationalism

Japan annexed Korea outright and made it a colony in 1910. Korea thus became a victim of imperialism. But unlike other such victims its master was a non-Western power. Whereas Christian missions and churches in other colonies were seen as part of the imperialist presence, in Korea the church was associated with a new nationalism. Christian leaders were prominent in societies organized to awaken Korean resistance to colonization. The church itself was seen by many as a refuge from Japanese rule. Its organization and networks posed political problems for the Japanese. Foreign missionaries wrote letters

[3]William Newton Blair, *Gold in Korea*, New York: Presbyterian Church in the U.S.A., 1957, pp.66–67.
[4]L. George Paik, *The History of Protestant Missions in Korea, 1832–1910*, Seoul: Yonsei University Press, 1970, p. 374.

home with frank reports about Japanese oppression. They also taught about freedom and democracy. Thus, from the start, the Japanese were apprehensive about Christianity in Korea. They set out to neutralize the church and to co-opt the missionaries.

The Japanese authorities dealt with the church in two major ways. The Government-General kept up a dialogue with the missionaries and impressed many with the reasonableness of its objectives in Korea, including religious toleration. But Korean Christians saw a different side of the regime. The *kempeitai*, or Japanese military police, singled out several Korean groups with names like "Self-Strengthening Society" and "New People's Society," accusing them of conspiracy to commit crimes. After a Korean nationalist assassinated Itō Hirobumi, the former Japanese resident-general, in 1909, such charges took on new meaning. In 1911 the *kempeitai* alleged that students at the Presbyterian school in Sŏnch'ŏn, in the northwest, had plotted to assassinate Governor-General Terauchi on a visit to the town. Many adults, mostly local Christians, were rounded up as co-conspirators. Missionaries were accused of having roused the students to action with chapel talks about David overcoming Goliath.

This incident, known as the Korean Conspiracy Case, led to a long trial. The main evidence was confessions, which some of the 123 defendants retracted in the courtroom, alleging that they had been extracted by torture. Most observers thought the case was a farce and eventually nearly all the defendants were released. Those who served time were granted amnesty in 1915. The most prominent of these, Yun Ch'i-ho, had been a leading Methodist educator, churchman and spokesman for independence. The experience was enough to keep him out of politics for the rest of his life. Thus the Conspiracy Case did succeed in intimidating many Christian activists and offered the church an incentive to stress the life of piety over the life of social action.

The Conspiracy Case was followed immediately by a series of orders from the Government-General requiring church institutions such as schools and hospitals to meet government standards for staffing and facilities. These included a requirement that religion not be part of regular school curriculum. This rule eliminated the raison d'être for most church and mission-related schools. At this point, churches virtually abandoned elementary education to the government. Higher academies were forced to teach religion after hours and, in some cases, off campus, generating a bitter dispute among the missionaries about whether or not they should be in education at all. Foreign and Korean church leaders together felt the pressure, and most missionaries came around to the view that the Japanese regime was an enemy of religious freedom.

**Christians in the March First Movement.** The March First 1919 Independence Movement was a pivotal event in modern Korean history.

The Korean Declaration of Independence proclaimed on that day had 33 signers, of whom 15 were Christians. Christians circulated copies of it underground. Christian groups organized rallies and demonstrations across the country. The fury of the *kempeitai* came down hard on the Christian community. Church leaders were rounded up; followers were beaten and shot; and in one instance, gendarmes locked a congregation inside a church and set it all ablaze, killing everyone within.[5] Clearly Christians were a target in the aftermath of the March First Movement, and the church suffered heavily. Yet it continued to grow despite this—or because of it, as some would argue, for the Korean church prides itself on its willingness to endure adversity.

**Christian intellectuals under Japanese rule.** During subsequent decades of Japanese rule the Korean church developed new maturity. The Y.M.C.A. was a Korean-run organization from the mid-1910s on. Seminary graduates staffed the churches and played a decisive role in the various denominations' governing bodies. Chōsen Christian College, an interdenominational project and predecessor of today's Yonsei University, became a center for intellectual life among Christians in Seoul. Korean Christians staffed the university faculty and occupied all the deanships by the mid-1930s. They embarked upon a study of Korean language and culture at a time when the Japanese were endeavoring to Japan-ize the Koreans. L. George Paik, then Dean of Humanities, sponsored a Korean studies institute. Ch'oe Hyŏn-bae, his colleague, worked out a new spelling system for Korean and helped found a society to preserve the language while the Japanese were trying to supress it. Before long the government ordered such scholars dismissed from their positions. Some even went to prison. But their activities as Christian faculty on the Christian college campus helped keep the church in the forefront of the resistance.

**The Catholic church under Japanese rule.** The Korean Catholic church grew relatively slowly until after World War II when it, too experienced an explosion in membership. Its nineteenth century history was rooted in persecution growing out of the fundamental conflict between Korean tradition—ancestor worship in particular—and Catholic doctrine.[6] After waves of repression, Korean Catholics finally won legal protection in 1886 through Korea's treaty with France, which guaranteed the safety of Catholic converts. This opened the way for legalization of all missionary work, both Catholic and Protestant.

Though progress for all Christian missionary work was slow in Korea

[5]Dae-yeol Ku, *Korea under Colonialism: The March First Movement and Anglo-Japanese Relations,* Seoul: Royal Asiatic Society, 1985, pp. 112–117.
[6]See Ch'oe Ki-bok, "The Abolition of Ancestral Rites and Tablets by Catholicism in the Chōson Dynasty and the Basic Meaning of Confucian Ancestral Rites," *Korean Journal,* August 1984, pp. 41–52. General information on Catholic missions and the Korean Catholic church in this report is derived from Joseph Chang-mun Kim and John Jae-sun Chung (eds.), *Catholic Korea Yesterday and Today,* Seoul: Catholic Korea Publishing Co., 1964, *passim.*

before the turn of the century and new congregations were few, the Catholics made conspicuous changes in the skyline of Seoul by erecting major churches at Yak-hyŏn and in Myŏng-dong. St Joseph's Church at Yak-hyŏn, which still stands a short distance from the Seoul railway station, was the first brick building in Korea. The Cathedral of the Immaculate Conception in Myŏng-dong, today the mother church of Korean Catholicism, was built on the site of the first Catholic meeting place in Korea, the home of Kim Pŏm-u, one of the earliest eighteenth century converts. Designed by Frenchmen and built under the supervision of Chinese contractors, it was consecrated in 1898. Some Koreans grumbled that the building's height—the steeple was 69 meters high—violated conventions forbidding construction of anything which could overlook the royal palace; but the king let it stand, partly because in the volatile international atmosphere of Korea he thought it best not to alienate the French.

Through the turn of the century, Catholic mission work was carried on primarily under the auspices of the Société des Missions-Étrangères de Paris (MEP), whose missioners managed the Catholic headquarters in Seoul. Their leader, Archbishop Auguste Mutel, presided over a vicariate which covered all of Korea and part of Manchuria. MEP fathers set up a seminary at Yongsan, Seoul, to train Korean priests. They also established a Catholic publishing house that published their translation of the Bible and a newspaper, the *Kyŏnghyang sinmun*, which, though shut down during the Japanese occupation, resumed publishing in 1945 and has been a leading daily paper ever since.

Another area of Catholic work was created in 1911 when Taegu became headquarters of Korea's second vicariate. Centering on the MEP cathedral and Convent of St. Paul de Chartres and the Seminary of St. Justin, the Taegu establishment supervised all Catholic work in the southern provinces of Kyŏngsang and Chŏlla until the 1930's, when the Chŏllas were subdivided into separate prefectures. During World War II the reigning French bishop at Taegu was forced to resign in favor of a Japanese priest. The Vatican appointed a Korean bishop in 1946, and the Catholic churches of the Taegu region have been under Korean control ever since.

As the years passed, the work of the French MEP fathers was augmented by the work of an international Catholic missionary force, whose different orders were assigned to different areas of the peninsula: German Benedictines in the northeast, American Maryknolls in the northwest and Irish Columbans in the southwest. The Benedictines arrived in 1909, under the leadership of Father Bonifatius Sauer. They first founded a monastery in Hyehwa-dong, Seoul. Since they were Germans, they suffered a period of suppression as enemies of the Japanese during World War I. After the war, they were given charge of the northeast, from Wŏnsan through the Hamgyŏng Provinces into Jiandao and all the way to Khabarovs. This area, known as the Vicariate of Yenchi (Korean: Yŏn'gil), was served between 1921 and 1941 by a German missionary body of 60 priests and 40 brothers, assisted by German and Swiss nuns. They made 35,000 converts, operated hospitals in Wŏnsan, Tŏgwŏn, Hamhŭng and Yenchi, and a seminary in Tŏgwŏn, as well as elementary schools and training centers for Korean nuns. The work of the Benedictines paralleled that of the Protestants, further strengthening the Christian church in northern Korea prior to World War II. In the war, since Germany and Japan were allies, Father (by then Bishop) Sauer and the German Benedictines were able to maintain their work after nearly all others were expelled. The end of that phase of Benedictine work came after the war, when North Korea came under communist rule and the missionaries were driven south to Taegu, where they have been since. Bishop Sauer, however, died in a Pyongyang prison in 1949, 40 years after founding the mission.

Northwestern Korea became the province for American Catholic work in 1923, with the arrival of the Maryknolls (from the Catholic Foreign Mission Society of America headquartered at Maryknoll, New York). They were assigned to work in the P'yŏngan Provinces, sharing the area with the American Northern Presbyterians. Building on the earlier work of the French MEP fathers, the Maryknollers established the Prefecture of Pyongyang in 1927, turning it over to Korean priests during World War II when they were expelled by the Japanese. At roughly the same time, the Chŏlla Provinces of southwestern Korea were separated from the vicariate of Taegu and assigned to a mission of Irish Columbans who arrived in the early 1930s. The Columbans established a new vicariate and seminary in Kwangju, South Chŏlla Province. North Chŏlla Province became a separate church prefecture entirely under Korean leadership in 1937.

By the eve of World War II the Catholic missionary societies operating in Korea could point to a number of successful institutions and a substantial number of converts—127,643 in 1937. Local leadership, however, was still quite weak. For a combination of reasons—territorial, organizational, financial and political—the Korean Catholic church was heavily dependent on foreign assistance, a condition which was not rectified for many years and which heightened the difficulties faced by Korean Catholics after 1945.

**The Korean church during World War II.** The Pacific War was a most traumatic time for all denominations of Korean Christians. As Japan expanded into Manchuria, then north China, and finally Southeast Asia, the Korean church faced grave tests.

Systematic pressure began in the mid-1930s with the Japanese Governor-General's order that all Koreans, as imperial subjects, should revere the emperor and the state by offering obeisance at Shintō shrines. The Government-General called it patriotic duty, and many Korean Christians simply went along. Indeed the Vatican, when asked to rule on the issue, affirmed that the shrine exercises were merely political and not religious, and that Korean Catholics had the duty to obey the laws of the state. Many Protestants, including majorities of several foreign missionary organizations, left it to individuals to decide as a matter of conscience. The Presbyterian establishment at Pyongyang, however, from the outset called it idolatry, setting the stage for a major confrontation between church and state, and also among members of the church who dissented from the views of the leadership.

When the Presbyterian General Assembly, while clearly under police coercion, voted in 1938 to define the Shintō ceremonies as non-religious, a serious rift opened between the Korean church and the missionaries. The missionaries denounced the assembly for its action and, as legal owners of the mission schools, voted to close the schools rather than to allow their students to participate in Shintō rituals. This in turn, alienated many Christian families, whose children's education was at stake. Congregations were bitterly torn. On one hand, the resisters, Korean and foreign, stood against the Japanese for God and Korea. On the other hand, the Presbyterian General Assembly could be charged with collaboration. The dispute took on a life of its own, as people traded accusations.

During World War II, the resisters suffered severe persecution and even martyrdom, while others who cooperated suffered comparatively little. By 1945, deep schisms had developed all across the Christian community that reflected conflicting strains of nationalism, religion and collaboration. In the emotions of the period just following the war, even questions of atonement and forgiveness became controversial. Charges bred countercharges, further complicated in later years by new pressures on the church imposed by communist rule in North Korea. The Shintō shrine issue can be taken as a starting point for the study of the fractiousness which is so evident in the Korean church today.

Many Catholic and virtually all Protestant missionaries left Korea before December 1941. After Pearl Harbor the compounds and school campuses owned by missionary organizations were commandeered as enemy property. All religious institutions, with the occasional exception of some belonging to the German Benedictines, were placed under Korean or Japanese management. In a real sense, devolution to local control was thus forced on the Korean churches. For those denominations that had already trained sufficient Korean leaders, this in itself posed little problem. The Catholic church, however, did not have enough Korean priests to staff all its parishes, and some were forced to close. Lay leaders who might have stepped into the breach were drafted into the Japanese army or forced to donate labor to the war effort.

The Korean church thus went into its own dark valley during the war years—its adherents harassed, many of its institutions closed, its leaders put under surveillance or in prison. In wartime church services the

Japanese required prayers for victory and collections for war materiel. Appointments for church positions required government approval. Leaders were required to write and broadcast appeals for loyalty to the Japanese Emperor's cause. Toward the end of the war, all Korean Christian sects were amalgamated into one unified church, as had been done in Japan. On the eve of Liberation Day, August 15, 1945, it was generally believed in Korea that the Japanese were preparing to go even further— that there were death lists with names of many of the country's Christians marked for execution.

When the Pacific War ended, Korea's Christians naturally were in the forefront of the celebration, for Japan's defeat meant liberation, and liberation was expected to mean religious toleration. For the moment, in August 1945, their joy was unbounded. But the celebration was short-lived. The victorious Allies divided Korea and occupied it. Religion came under attack almost immediately in Russian-occupied North Korea. And in churches all over Korea, bitter disputes erupted between those who had collaborated with the Japanese and those who had resisted. Just as the rebirth of Korea following liberation from Japan meant a rebirth of the Korean church, the ordeal of Korea in the years which followed brought new ordeals for the church as well.

# III. Development of the Korean Church, 1945–1961

## Liberation and the Korean War

In 1945, Korea was liberated from Japan only to be occupied by Soviet and American troops who eventually divided their country into incompatible halves. The Soviet Union had joined the war against Japan on the eve of victory, and advanced so quickly through Manchuria that the American military command was obliged to propose a joint occupation of Korea, the zone north of the 38th parallel for the Soviets, the zone south of the line, including the capital, for the Americans. To this the Soviets agreed.

The 38th parallel was not meant to be a national or political boundary. It was understood that Soviet-American negotiations would lead to a coalition government under which Korea could be reunited as an independent state. But the negotiations broke down, and by 1947 the border had become nearly impenetrable. In 1948 Koreans on both sides established governments, after which the occupation forces pulled out. In Seoul, an American-educated Methodist named Syngman Rhee became president of the Republic of Korea (R.O.K.), created under sponsorship of the United Nations. In Pyongyang, Kim Il Sung, a Soviet-trained military officer, took charge of the communist Democratic People's Republic of Korea (D.P.R.K.). Each sought to overthrow the other. Northern-backed guerrillas fomented rebellion in the south with mixed results but requiring much repression. Finally the D.P.R.K. abandoned the insurrectionist policy in favor of outright conquest, and on June 25, 1950, it launched an invasion.

In retrospect it seems clear that the North Korean invasion was a terrible miscalculation. The Pyongyang regime believed that the United States had left Syngman Rhee to fend for himself and would not interfere with its conquest of the south. But the Truman Administration decided to make Korea a test case of the policy of containing communist expansionism. Through the United Nations the United States created an international military force under the command of General Douglas MacArthur to roll back the invasion. By October 1950 this objective had been achieved. But then the United Nations forces also miscalculated, pressing north to destroy the Pyongyang regime. To preserve Kim Il Sung's government and to protect their border, the Chinese communists then intervened, forcing the U.N. army back to the 38th parallel. Two years of truce talks then followed, leading to an armistice, which was finally signed in July 1953.

This was merely a ceasefire, in effect an interruption in the fighting, and technically the war is still in progress. This fact is basic to the political culture of both halves of Korea today. It is why both sides maintain such enormous military forces. And as a result, except for a symbolic exchange of visitors in 1985, citizens have never been allowed to cross

15

the line or even to exchange mail since the Korean War. Broadcasts are still jammed; news is censored; and 30 years after the 1953 truce there are still many families who do not know whether relatives a few miles away are alive or dead.

The Korean War prevented the communization of South Korea. But the price was terrible. An estimated 2.8 million Koreans died in the war along with 50,889 U.N. troops, of whom 33,629 were Americans.[7] The war ruined the cities and economies of both sides and reduced both states to dependence on the superpowers for a quarter of a century. Both economies are now fully reconstructed, with the south surpassing the north in growth, exports and per capita income. Both sides profess a desire for reunification but are slow to conciliate, and there is little reason to hope that they can reach an accommodation. Rather, each government relies on fear of the other side to justify its policies. Nothing must be allowed to undermine state security. Legitimate dissent—an opposition political party seeking to replace the party in power, for example—is easy to construe as a threat to national security and to be strictly controlled. Thus the legacy of the Korean War continues to stunt political development in the south, even though economic progress has brought great gains in the material quality of life.

### The Effect of National Division on the Church

Since Liberation in 1945, the Korean church has had a stormy history. Protestants and Catholics both suffered terribly in North Korea before and during the war. By 1949, Christian congregations in North Korea had been shattered and major church establishments, such as the Benedictine mission station at Wŏnsan and the Christian institutions of Pyongyang, were experiencing great difficulties and persecution. Although Kim Il Sung himself had been reared in a churchgoing family, by the time he came to power he was thoroughly opposed to the Christian faith and its links to "imperialism." By 1949 his regime had succeeded in crushing the booming Christian movement that once had been centered in his capital city.

As the 38th parallel hardened into a political boundary between 1945 and 1949, Christians joined the spectacular exodus to the south. For the American-backed government of Syngman Rhee in Seoul it was a major propaganda coup. From the refugees' point of view, life under the Methodist Rhee could not but be better than under the Marxist Kim Il Sung. Leading Christians in the north had been arrested and some had disappeared without a trace. Likewise, in areas of South Korea that experienced several communist-led insurrections in 1948–49, Christians fared badly as alleged "running dogs" of American and Japanese imperialism and enemies of the people. The Korean War exacerbated all

---

[7]David Rees, *Korea: The Limited War*, Baltimore: Penguin Books, 1964, pp. 460–461.

16

this and hardened forever the enmity of Christians for the northern regime. Christians in areas occupied by invading communist troops were often killed. The missionary community also suffered, as foreign workers were captured and forced to march from camp to camp in North Korea, an ordeal that caused many deaths. The entire experience served to heighten the tradition of martyrdom in the Korean churches and drew the Christians of Korea even closer together. It is the reason why Christianity and communism are mortal enemies in Korea, and it helps explain why the majority of the Korean church—Catholic and Protestant—is loyal to the anti-communist government in Seoul, and why the government, in turn, invites and welcomes church support. The Korean War hardened forever the enmity of Christians for the northern regime.

## The Return of the Missionaries

The end of World War II and the liberation of Korea reopened opportunities for missionary work in South Korea. Many missionaries returned after 1946 with the permission of the U.S. military occupation authorities. They found a troubled church still divided over the conflicts of the Japanese colonial period. The wartime Methodist bishop, for example, was under attack for leading prayers for a Japanese victory and selling church land and taking offerings to raise funds for weapons and aircraft. Liberation meant disgrace for him and purges for his followers. Yun Ch'i-ho, Korea's leading Methodist layman, died in 1945 while still under criticism for his public statements in support of Japan.

The General Assembly of the Presbyterian Church, which had buckled under Japanese pressure in 1938 and voted to obey the Japanese orders regarding Shintō shrine worship, was torn apart after the war when those who had resisted—and survived—attacked those who had given in. the issues were not only theological: they were also personal and took on the look of witch hunts within the church.

Into this maelstrom of church politics came the returning missionaries. They wished to heal and restore the church to what it had been before the mid-1930s; i.e., to resume their old positions of authority. But many of their Korean counterparts had different ideas.

One issue was property ownership. The foreign missionary boards held title to considerable institutional land in Korea and believed it to be theirs. Many Korean churchmen argued that in an independent Korea the time had come for devolution of the property to the local church. For example, Chōsen Christian University ("Yonsei" today) had been seized by the Japanese as enemy property during the war. In 1945, well before the return of the missionary trustees, the Korean faculty took possession of the campus, elected a Korean president, and resumed instruction.

Then came the question of financing. The mission board in New York

17

held the endowment and was reluctant to forward the proceeds to a governing body they did not control. It maintained this position for three years, until there were missionaries on the scene. This seemed high-handed to the Koreans and signaled the apparent intention of the missionaries and their home churches to reestablish the patron-client relationship of bygone years.

The patron-client issue would have been much more explosive under other circumstances. South Korea, after all, was under American military rule until 1948 and it was impolitic to be overtly anti-American. The economy was nearly wrecked by the sudden divorce from Japan and further, by the division of the agricultural South from the more industrialized North. The people themselves were in shock over the partitioning of their nation, and the church was fighting for survival. Even though the returning missionaries were paternalistic at times, they were important to the church as supporters and protectors. It was natural—even desireable—to let them resume positions of authority and not to rush the issue of devolution. The Korean War further increased the dependence of the church on foreign assistance.

The war brought Korea to the attention of many foreign missionary bodies that had never shown any interest before, and numerous new missionaries arrived in Korea to start new denominations after 1953. Many of these are still actively involved in training Korean followers, and while the old denominations are independent of foreign funding and control, the newer missionary organizations are still growing and pumping funds into the country. It cannot be said, therefore, that the Korean church is completely free of missionary influence, even though the Koreans themselves govern their churches and have been sending their own workers abroad for more than a generation.

During the 1950s, Korea began digging out from under the rubble of war. This was made possible by the grim determination of the survivors and by massive infusions of government and private aid from the outside. Overseas Christians and their representatives in Korea contributed much to this effort. President Syngman Rhee, a member of the First Methodist Church in Seoul, supported the church and wished it well. Many of his closest associates were Christians and much was said about the Christianization of South Korea while he was president. North Korean exiles founded many new churches of their own in the South, dealing with the special needs of refugees and swelling the membership lists.

Though welcome, North Koreans were still outsiders. Those from the church's old heartland in the northwest brought with them their reputation for competitiveness. Their ultra-conservative theology, inculcated by the early fundamentalist missionaries, did not always wear well in the South; nor did their air of martyrdom and special spirituality, which came from toughing it out against the Japanese over the shrine question and surviving the communist takeover of their home provinces.

It is hardly surprising, therefore, that after a few years new stresses built up in the church. These exploded in 1959 when the annual meeting of the Presbyterian General Assembly broke up in a combination of struggles over delegates' credentials, regional rivalries and theology (e.g., Moses' authorship of the Pentateuch, the divine inspiration of scripture, and the place of women in the church). A further issue was the Korean National Christian Council's membership in the World Council of Churches, which some deemed to be a communist front. Back of it all lay the old struggle over Shintō worship, the legacy of Japanese rule, and the role of missionaries, who tried to heal the meeting but were swept aside instead. Two denominations of nearly equal size emerged from the meeting, and in neither did foreign missionaries exercise control. From that point forward it was clear to everyone that the Korean Presbyterian church had set its own course and was completely independent.

# IV. Main Currents of Christianity in Korea

Korean Christianity today may be described in terms of institutions, trends and contradictions. Christian churches and related institutions are independent of missionaries, though perhaps arguably not free of foreign influence. The Korean church is growing very fast and evolving its own theology—or, more properly, theologies. And it is struggling with the issues posed by Korea's unique heritage, present political position, and rapid economic development.

Korean Christians are rightly proud of their growth in numbers. Publicity about this phenomenon usually is illustrated by photographs of outdoor services in the vast plaza on Yŏido Island. Here over the years millions of Koreans have gathered to hear visiting evangelical leaders such as Dr. Billy Graham. A million or more Korean Catholics turned out in the square in May 1984 to celebrate their bicentennial in a special mass led by the visiting Pope John Paul II. Such scenes recall Chinese Cultural Revolution rallies in Beijing's Tiananmen Square during the 1960s, and they suggest the strength of Christianity as a cultural and even political force in modern Korea.

The church in Korea has now fully devolved to Korean control. The Protestant denominations that developed for the most part under missionary guidance prior to World War II are now completely controlled by Korean governing bodies in which few, if any, foreigners have a voice. The Catholic church since 1962 has been under a Korean archbishop (now cardinal). This is not to say that the missionaries are completely gone; rather they work in and for Korean church organizations, doing things Koreans think they should do.

The autonomy of the Korean church is partly the result of conscious missionary policies. For example, at the turn of the century the Presbyterians, who comprised the largest missionary body, adopted a program to foster self-propagation, self-government and self-support. This was the Nevius plan, named for John L. Nevius, the Presbyterian China missionary who devised it.[8] It opened unheard-of opportunities for common people, women and men, to enjoy social and educational advancement through participation in the church. It spurred modernization through literacy programs and leadership training. It also emphasized rigid adherence to doctrine and strict rules for Christian behavior, which led to much hair-splitting later on. Some say that its emphasis on a Korean-trained pastorate put a barrier between the missionaries, who generally had advanced liberal educations from America and Europe, and their Korean colleagues, who had to make do with

---

[8]See Charles Allen Clark, *The Korean Church and the Nevius Methods,* New York: Fleming H. Revell Co., 1930.

narrow religious training in the local seminary. Today, whether the Nevius plan is credited for Presbyterian strengths or blamed for its weaknesses, there is no doubt that it was one of the main factors in spreading a particularly conservative faith throughout the peninsula.

Theological and political conservatism characterizes the ideology of mainstream Korean Christianity. This conservatism comes from Korean tradition and draws on Confucian principles of hierarchy, authority and orthodoxy. It is reinforced by the pietistic religious tradition introduced by the Protestant missionaries, by the history of trials that the church has suffered, and by a strong anti-communism born of the country's experience with the 38th parallel and the Korean War.

Manifestations of church conservatism include a strong leader orientation in congregations whose loyalty to the pastor often exceeds loyalty to the organized denomination. The heart of any church naturally is its membership; but many of Korea's denominational churches are actually congregational rather than denominational, focused on local concerns rather than on denomination-wide projects, or issues of concern to society as a whole.

Another trait is the theological rigidity that appears in doctrinal disagreements, which sometimes are little more than basic struggles among factions. Orthodoxy is reinforced by frequent group Bible study in which scriptural issues are discussed in fine detail, strengthening group beliefs. It also infuses believers with a strong sense of shared spirituality and evangelistic fervor. But the sharing can also cross congregational and even denominationsl lines, as during Korea's periodic mega-crusades. At one of the largest of these, the 1980 "Here's Life, Korea!" campaign, for example, it is said that one and a half million Christians representing the spectrum of theological viewpoints passed each night of the crusade in Yōido Plaza praying together for the evangelization of their country.[9]

The results comprise a paradox. Christianity in Korea is factionridden over doctrinal, historical and political issues, and depends heavily on pastoral leadership. And yet it, claims many followers, displays vital forces for growth, and is capable of impressive displays of unity.

### History, Theology and Society in Korea: Two Examples
One way to understand the appeal of Korean Christianity, or more specifically the functioning of the Protestant majority, is to look at two of the most prominent congregations in Seoul: the Yōngnak Church, a North Korean refugee congregation whose organization and theology is fundamentally that of the Protestant church since its inception a cen-

---

[9]Kim Joon-Gon, "Korea's Total Evangelization Movement," in Ro Bong-Rin and Marlin L. Nelson editors, *Korean Church Growth Explosion*, Seoul: Word of Life Press, 1983, pp. 17–50.

tury ago, and whose members have banded together to survive the vicissitudes of modern Korean history; and the Central Full Gospel Church on Yŏido Island, an evangelistic phenomenon which has grown up entirely in the cultural and psychological milieu of postwar Korea.

**Yŏngnak Presbyterian Church.**[10] Yŏngnak Church dates from 1946, when it was founded by Han Kyŏng-jik, a refugee Presbyterian minister from Sinŭiju far in the northwest on the Chinese border. Han was a protégé of the Presbyterian establishment at Pyongyang, having attended Union Christian College there and then Princeton Theological Seminary in the United States. The Japanese forced him out of his first pastorate in Sinŭiju, and he spent the war years operating a home for abandoned children and old people near that town.

When the war ended, Liberation quickly turned sour for the Christians of Sinŭiju. Russian occupation authorities began harassing and arresting Christian ministers almost immediately. Han saw several of his colleagues led away; he himself headed south to the American zone. When he reached Seoul in October 1945 he found other Sinŭiju refugees, including members of his old church, in the city. Their group became the nucleus of the Yŏngnak congregation.

By the spring of 1946, Yŏngnak had 500 members. Han Kyŏng-jik got the permission of the American occupation authorities to use the confiscated property of the Shintō sect of Tenrikyō for his church. In 1948, after it was plain that the Yŏngnak congregation was not going to be able to return home to Sinŭiju, Han began a permanent building. His own refugees raised $60,000 and he got $20,000 more from American donors. The congregation then set about constructing the 2,500-seat stone sanctuary building with their own labor. Two years later it was finished, and the dedication was held on June 4, 1950. Three weeks later the Korean War began.

The war forced Yŏngnak's members to become refugees again. Some of them relocated in Taegu and Pusan, where they formed mutual aid networks and continued to gather members. The U.N. forces' short-lived occupation of North Korea late in 1950 enabled the southward escape of thousands more northern Christians, many of whom were assisted by Yŏngnak members. After the war they returned to Seoul, repaired their building and began to rebuild their lives. The congregation raised funds for a school for the deaf, several orphanages, a middle school and a boys' high school. Multiple services on Sundays could not handle the membership, so annexes were built onto the sanctuary building. Closed-circuit television carried services into adjacent audito-

[10]Harold E. Fey, "A Great Church in Seoul," *The Christian Century,* December 26, 1952, pp. 1506–1510; Samuel Hugh Moffett, *The Christians of Korea,* New York: Friendship Press, 1962, pp. 21–25; Park Cho-Choon, "The Dynamics of Young Nak Presbyterian Church Growth," in Ro and Nelson, *op. cit.,* pp. 201 210.

riums, with simultaneous translation into several different languages for foreign visitors.

Today Yŏngnak has 60,000 members, 22 ordained pastors and 24 lay ministers, seven choirs, and five services each Sunday. Han Kyong-jik, though retired, still preaches from time to time. It has long since ceased to be a refugee church and embraces many southerners as well. The pastoral staff estimates growth at ten percent per year, and despite the continual establishment of subsidiary "daughter" congregations elsewhere in the city, the projected membership for the mother congregation in 1990 is 100,000. This has led to plans to build a new 10,000-seat sanctuary across the Han River to the south of the city.

Yŏngnak Church, though larger than most, is typical of Korean Protestantism in several ways. Its roots, in the person of Han Kyong-jik, go back before World War II. It is keenly aware of Korea as a whole-not-divided country, and of the church's dynamic first half-century. Its theology is conservative, stressing the will and power of God, the sinful estate of man, salvation of individuals through grace and redemption through Christ (i.e., being "born again"), and the communion of believers. Sermons focus on the Bible and on understanding the Christian life as a spiritual state. Leaders concern themselves with individual members and on involving them in networks of fellowship and mutual support within the church. They also urge them out into the community with exhortations to witness through Godly lives. Participation, therefore, is a key element in Yŏngnak's growth and dynamism, affording members a sense of purpose beyond their own material well-being.

If, as it is sometimes proposed, the cause of Korea's present malaise is not the North Korean threat or the ordeal of modernization but the discrediting of the old Confucian wellsprings of value, then churches such as Yŏngnak—and there are many, both Catholic and Protestant—may be succeeding because they offer an alternative tradition that seems to the church members themselves to belong to *them*, with roots in their own history. This seems like a paradox in a church so heavily influenced by foreign missionaries at various stages. The explanation lies in the fact that the missionaries never could become Koreans and, as foreigners and with few exceptions, have never been able fully to share in the experiences of their Korean co-believers.

**The Central Full Gospel Church on Yŏido Island.**[11] The Central Full Gospel Church claims to be the largest congregation in the world. As of September 1983 it had 325,421 members and is, in effect, a denomination unto itself. Its founder, Paul Yŏnggi Cho, became a Christian in 1956 when, he says, he was healed of terminal tuberculosis through the visits and prayers of an itinerant Biblewoman. After a period in the

---

[11]*Korea Calling*, (Seoul), October 1968; Paul Yonggi Cho and John W. Hurston, "Ministry through Home Cell Units," in Ro and Nelson, *op. cit.*, pp. 270–289.

Assemblies of God Bible Institute in Seoul he started leading open-air meetings and doing faith healing on his own. By 1961 he had a proper church building, and by 1968 the church had a congregation of five thousand. Growth has been exponential ever since, and when Korean Christians use the word "explosion" to describe their movement, it is Paul Cho's church that first comes to mind.

It is to Cho's credit that the Full Gospel Church is not a one-man show. It began that way, but Cho suffered a physical breakdown in 1964, which taught him to delegate leadership within his organization. Building on a missionary colleague's concept of lay leadership and Wesleyan-style class meetings, or cells, in homes, he created elaborate networks of authority within the congregation. Cell leaders—many of whom have the "gift of tongues"—attend classes and then teach the cell members. Cell members then go out and recruit new members. The church makes full use of television and publishes a magazine of its own, *The World of Faith*, and a congregational newspaper, *The Full Gospel News*. Copies of *The Full Gospel News* are distributed all over Seoul.

It is the spectacular services, most of all, which characterize the Full Gospel Church. The vast auditorium on Yŏido is a beehive of organization and excitement, with buses and automobiles jamming the streets outside. The congregation sings with gusto and inspiration, and when Cho speaks, the sheer magnitude of his operation calls forth reverence. The visitor cannot help but be moved by what has been accomplished.

Some of the criticism of the Central Full Gospel Church is pure jealousy. The church is popular and its members are aggressive in their personal evangelism. But there is something deeper which disturbs many Korean Christians. Son Bong-ho, a philosophy professor at Han'guk Theological Seminary, calls it "a fatal lack of critical attitude toward the materialism of modern culture."[12]

Indeed, Paul Cho's message is one that stresses God's material blessings in the present life. The church slogan is from the second verse of the third epistle of John: "Beloved, I pray that all may go well with you and that you may be in health; I know that it is well with your soul." This leads to the church's "triple-meter faith" in riches of the spirit, of the body, and in possessions. Much of the praying focuses on daily problems, and daily problems invariably involve money.

It also involves praying for security from a North Korean attack and for preservation of the South Korean state. There is a patriotic fervor and an emphasis on Korea as Asia's first Christian nation, God's chosen people and instrument. The power of positive thinking, mixing religion and patriotism, has reached Korea and has found a following.

Paul Cho's Central Full Gospel Church is part of the fastest growing wing of Korean Christendom. Where old-line Protestants of the type

[12]Son Bong-Ho, "Some Dangers of Rapid Growth," in Ro and Nelson, *op cit.*, pp. 337–338.

represented by Yŏngnak Church stay close to an austere Korean fundamentalism rooted in the Bible and modern Korean history, and dissident *Minjung* theologians appeal to the working class with an emerging Korean-style Christianity based on the traditions of Korea and the suffering of her people, the middle-class Pentecostals of the Full Gospel Church accentuate the positive and preach miracles, attracting tens of thousands with promises of a better life tomorrow. Some say that the ministers of this charismatic religion are simply latter-day shamans who offer a cheap faith, raid other churches for members, and promise God's blessings in material terms. This may be true, but for the emerging bourgeoisie of Korea with its eminently material concerns, Paul Cho's gospel offers irresistible attractions.

### Organization and Leadership of the Korean Church

Pastors Han Kyŏng-jik and Paul Cho, representatives of the two main strains—conservative and ultra-evangelical—of Korean Protestant leadership, share characteristics with a succession of church leaders over the years who have started out as products of missionary-sponsored training institutes and have gone on to build careers entirely devoted to Korean pastorates, with no organizational ties to foreign mission bodies. Their tradition of independent local leadership is one that all Christian sects in Korea have emphasized from the beginning.

It started with the early French Catholics, who lost no time preparing a Korean pastorate. Andrew Kim Tae-gŏn, the first Catholic priest, was sent to Macao to study for his ordination in 1836. The early Presbyterians ordained their first Korean elders in 1887, established their seminary at Pyongyang in 1901, and ordained their first ministers in 1907. The Methodists were not far behind, founding their seminary in 1910.

The original aim of all mission schooling in Korea at the turn of the century was to prepare a generation of local leaders for the church. The first Protestant college in Pyongyang was really a Bible institute run by a combination of denominations and was intended to train future seminarians. The demand for a broader modern education soon forced the mission schools to liberalize the curriculum, but theological training programs continued strong and are important on all Christian college campuses to this day.

At present, all the major sects and denominations have seminaries. These graduate thousands of students each year. Most are undergraduate seminaries, that is, theological schools offering a core of religious studies that may lead either to regular degrees or to further divinity training and eventual ordination. Under current rules for undergraduate institutions set forth by the Ministry of Education, the undergraduate seminaries resemble regular colleges, and they are subject to the same kinds of problems as ordinary schools.

Individual congregations often seem to take little responsibility for financing their denominational seminaries. Endowments are rare, and most schools are obliged to struggle along on tuition income. Facilities and faculty are often below average. Because the students are younger, because in many cases they are there because they failed to get into the college of their choice, and because seminary campuses, like all campuses, are heavily politicized and feature frequent strikes and student demonstrations, Korean seminaries do not possess the rarefied atmosphere that Americans might expect to find at, say Yale Divinity School.

Prior to 1950, virtually all holders of advanced theology degrees in Korea acquired them abroad, mostly in Japan and the United States. In 1957, Yonsei University started a United Graduate School of Theology, which was intended to offer advanced training to candidates from all the major Protestant sects. Drawing on the Yonsei faculty and on part-time teaching by seminary professors from across the city, it stood alone until the major denominations instituted graduate programs of their own. The rush to set up sectarian graduate programs may be seen as a bandwagon phenomenon, but it was also a sign of the maturity and independence of the Korean church in general.

The main interdenominational organization in Korea is the National Christian Council (N.C.C.), an outgrowth of the Federal Council of Churches and Missions, which was founded in 1916. The N.C.C. has served as a link with the international church, has sponsored numerous evangelistic conferences and crusades in Korea, and has underwritten the management of a number of interfaith projects such as the Christian Broadcasting System, the Christian Literature Society, social services for Koreans living in Japan, and a wide-ranging educational program, which includes audio-visual materials and publication of Sunday school literature. The Council is ecumenical in outlook and is affiliated with the World Council of Churches. Its main critic is a Presbyterian federation associated with the ultraconservative World Evangelical Fellowship (formerly the National Association of Evangelicals). This group continually accuses the N.C.C. of political and theological leftism and denounces its ties to the World Council. Nevertheless, after 25 years of wrangling and competition, both federations may still be seen as conservative, upright, anti-communist and patriotic. In practice there is considerable cooperation between them.

## Women in the Church

Ever since the 1780s, women have been a cornerstone of the church. Numerous women are to be found among the 103 Catholic martyrs canonized by Pope John Paul II in May 1984. Catholic institutions of all types owe a great deal to the work of sister communities, even though nuns often were scorned, especially in the beginning, because of their choice to remain unmarried.[13] The Protestants' Nevius plan stressed the cultivation of Christian women, encouraged their participation in Bible classes and church activities and sought, above all, to make them keepers of Christian homes, devotedly rearing Christian children. This was the early missionaries' response to the greater resistance encountered among men in general, and upper-class men in particular. The importance of women in the early church was instantly obvious to anyone visiting during services, for men and women sat on opposite sides of the aisle, and the women's side invariably was much better filled. This preponderance of women in church is still visible in many places, borne out by church statistics across Korea that show that in the 1980s three-fourths of Korea's Christians are women.[14]

There are many reasons for this. Women traditionally have embraced religious practice in Korea more readily than men (for example, in Buddhist temple worship, where the same disproportion of women is apparent). Another reason is that the Christian church from the beginning offered women historic new opportunities for growth and self-expression, which no Korean religion had ever offered before.

In the church hierarchy women were welcome as Sunday school teachers and lay workers ("Biblewomen"), and were often elected to middle-level governing bodies such as boards of deacons. To prepare them for leadership positions in the church, the various denominations founded girls' schools which offered them education for the first time. These quickly grew and developed into modern institutions, which in turn opened other careers for them as well, in higher education, medicine and other technical fields. Ewha Women's University, founded in 1886 by Mary B. Scranton of the Methodist Mission, is the prime example of this massive educational effort. There women learned to read and solve problems; they learned history and English and democratic principles; and their senses were sharpened to the issues of justice and opportunity for women. The Confucian tradition placed (and still places) women at a disadvantage in many aspects of life; the progress made possible for them within and through the Christian church was nothing short of revolutionary.[15] But it was also to be expected that becoming aware of the inequalities suffered by women historically would cause many Christian women to demand that the church do better: that it grant them governing authority within the church and not confine their role to one of nurturing Christian children.

[13]Kim Ok-hy, "Women in the History of Catholicism in Korea," *Korea Journal*, August 1984, pp. 28–40.
[14]Lee Youn-Ok, "The Role of Women in Korean Church Growth," in Ro and Nelson, *op. cit.*, p. 238.
[15]Kee Tiyb-Ok, op. cit., pp. 230–244; Yung-chung Kim, editor, *Women of Korea: a History from Ancient Times to 1945*, Seoul: Ewha Womans University Press, 1979, pp. 195–212; and Kim Ok-hy, "Women in the History of Catholicism in Korea," *Korea Journal*, August 1984, pp. 28–40.

Indeed, church women have become restive under the customary restraints that prevent their taking full responsibility for leadership in the church. A recent poll among Presbyterians asked why women could not be ordained. Forty-one percent said it was because of "the traditional custom of men's superiority complex." Twenty-six percent said that ordination of women was contrary to the scriptures. Fourteen percent listed various other reasons, such as "not a proper time, yet." In fact, more and more women are taking administrative positions in educational institutions and bureaus of the church. They are among the most insistent that further opportunities be opened for equality, and they warn that if this does not happen soon the church "will suffer from the loss of these talented and capable workers. The church's evangelistic outreach will be greatly reduced by this loss."[16] Given Pope John Paul II's responses to American churchwomen requesting admission to the priesthood, there is little reason to expect much change for Catholic women in Korea. But even the most democratic Protestant churches have structures that are strongly (if not always consciously) patriarchal. There is little reason to hope that Korean churches can do much better than those in other countries in admitting women to traditionally male positions.

## Church Outreach

**Church institutions.** Since the days of the early missionaries, the church has divided its efforts among evangelism, education, medicine and social welfare. Church-sponsored educational institutions today are among Korea's best. The most elaborate is Yonsei University, formed in 1957 by the union of Yŏnhi University (formerly Chōsen Christian College, founded 1915) and Severance Union Medical College, which grew out of a tiny mission clinic founded in 1885. At the time of its centennial in May 1985, Yonsei had over 30,000 students and 789 faculty in 15 colleges and seven graduate schools. Near Yonsei is Ewha Women's University, founded by Methodist women and now the largest women's university in Asia. Nearby, too, is Sŏgang University, founded in 1960 by a team of Jesuits from Wisconsin and known throughout Korea for its academic quality. Other Christian colleges and universities are to be found throughout Korea, including Kyemyŏng University in Taegu and Hannam and Mogwŏn Colleges in Taejŏn. Sungjon University, which is descended from Pyongyang's prewar Union Christian College, was reestablished in Seoul after the war by North Korean Christians who had come south.

As with schools, so with hospitals: Korean Christians are engaged in a wide variety of medical work. The Catholic Medical Center in Seoul is a major installation, as are the Presbyterian hospitals in Chŏnju, Taegu,

[16]Lee Youn-Ok, *op. cit.*, pp. 239–240.

and Pusan. These centers have brought innovations to medical care in Korea, such as the creation of satellite clinics in outlying towns and rural public health stations in remote areas such as Kŏje Island. As they expand they take on more free clinic work in urban neighborhoods, providing a valuable supplement to government welfare programs.

**Community involvement.** It would be hard to exaggerate the impact of local churches on their communities. Evangelical churches expect their members to invite neighbors and friends to services; children in the Sunday schools are urged to bring their friends with them. Churches sometimes provide space for kindergartens and day-care centers, or for community meetings, weddings, and other celebrations.

Along with the churches themselves are related organizations such as the YMCA and YWCA, both of which have active social and sports programs for young people. The Kagyo ("Bridge") theater company tours the country performing plays with Christian themes. The Korean Bible Society, the Christian Literature Society, and the Gideons make sure there is plenty of Christian reading-matter. Chaplains in all branches of the military service minister to men in uniform. The Korean branch of the German-founded Christian Academy movement provides a place for intellectuals to gather and discuss current issues. Christian Businessmen's Associations put on Kiwanis-style lunch meetings and invite coworkers to hear Christian speakers. At other times they organize prayer breakfasts and invited public officials to join them in prayers for the peace and welfare of the state.

The Korean church contributes much to welfare work. The Korean War made this a necessary emphasis of missionary programs in Korea, but some of what the missionaries started continues under Korean church sponsorship. Orphanages continue to care for abandoned children, orphans, and children from desperately poor families. The Maryknoll-sponsored Sacred Heart School for the Blind is one of many church-related blind schools. The Wilson Leprosy Center and Rehabilitation Hospital in Sunch'on is one of several centers for victims of leprosy. The House of Grace near Yonsei University offers shelter, counseling and alternative job-training for women who want to get out of prostitution. The Methodist church cooperates in a legal aid program that works with family courts to protect women who have little protection from abuse under the traditional social system. Catholic dioceses have begun marriage counseling programs, which have been very successful among young urban professionals. All these projects are funded by Koreans, with little but symbolic aid from abroad. Yŏngnak Church dedicates a special collection on the last Sunday of each month to support the congregation's social welfare programs: a program for the deaf, a shelter for women, a home for the elderly, and an education program that includes a Christian middle school, a girls' school and a women's seminary. In traditional Korea, charity began at home. The church has multiplied and extended it to strangers as an expression of Christian commitment.

**Student ministries.** Korea's colleges and universities enroll more than a million students. They are determined to get educations that will admit them to elite jobs and status, and many have little time for anything but study. But a conspicuous minority are active in political movements, and of these, a highly visible number are involved in the protest movement. Since 1960, when students succeeded in generating a popular revolution against the regime of Syngman Rhee, universities have been breeding grounds for confrontations with the government. Though the issues change, the atmosphere on the major campuses is charged with political ideas, rumors, and plans for action.

Although political protest seems to be the main extracurricular activity on campus, involving Christian and non-Christian students alike, many of Korea's colleges and universities have active campus ministries that seek to relate the gospel message to student concerns. Chapters of Christian youth organizations may be found in secular as well as religious schools. these are of different types: home-grown Korean organizations (e.g., the JOY Mission, founded in 1958; the University Bible Fellowship, founded in 1961; and the Student Bible Fellowship, founded in 1976), and local branches of international organizations (e.g., Campus Crusade for Christ, established in 1958; Korea Inter-Varsity Christian Fellowship, est. 1959; Youth for Christ, est. 1961; and The Navigators, est. 1966). Local chapters choose their own leaders, are usually interdenominational, and center on regular meetings in which members study passages of the Bible and discuss current problems in light of the scripture. They also serve an important social purpose, widening friendships through recruiting and group recreation such as hikes, picnics and talent shows.

Some Christian student organizations express themselves in social service projects, such as providing child care to farmers during the busiest planting season, teaching country people to read, or leading services temporarily in churches that are searching for ministers. Some even send students abroad on work camp projects or quasi-missionary enterprises.[17]

Other Christian organizations are deeply involved in the student protest movement. During the May 1985 student demonstrations commemorating the 1980 Kwangju Incident, for example, underground handbills calling the regime to account for the incident were signed by the Korea Christian Youth Federation, the Alliance of Korean Christian Student Organizations, and the Korea Catholic University Students' League.

[17]Ro and Nelson, *op. cit.*, p. 122ff.; p. 322ff.

Thus Christian student organizations reflect the spectrum of opinion and emphasis within the church. They are devout; their religion is strongly Bible-oriented; they are active in social service; and a minority are involved in radical political causes.

**Mass communication.** The early missionaries faced formidable difficulties in conveying the Christian message to the Korean people. Though their spoken language is grammatically unrelated to Chinese, Koreans traditionally used Chinese characters almost exclusively until the turn of the century. There was an easy-to-learn alphabet for Korean called ŏnmun ("vulgar writing"), which could have been used to write vernacular Korean, but it was denigrated by the educated aristocracy. Thus, virtually all Korean books were published in the more elegant—and difficult—classical Chinese. Most Koreans could not afford training in classical Chinese, and were therefore, in effect, illiterate.

The simple ŏnmun alphabet appealed to the missionaries because it *was* simple. It seemed the ideal medium for religious literature since foreigners could learn it almost as easily as ordinary Koreans. Thus, the Bible, which was already available in Chinese, was translated into Korean onmun, with far-reaching implications. The churches carried on literacy campaigns to encourage the use of ŏnmun among churchgoers. Gospels, tracts and Sunday school materials were snapped up by "illiterate" Koreans outside the church who enjoyed the feeling of being able to read. Some of them got the message and joined the church. Ŏnmun became especially popular all across Korea during the Japanese colonial period, when the use of the native Korean alphabet acquired a patriotic meaning. Linguists refined it and standardized the spelling so that it could be used with, or instead of, Chinese characters. After 1945 it became known by its more dignified name of Han'gŭl. National leaders recognized its importance for education and modernization, and today the use of Han'gŭl is standard in both North and South Korea.

After World War II, the missionaries turned to radio to spread the Christian message across Korea. The Christian Broadcasting System (CBS), whose development had been postponed by the Korean War, began transmitting in 1954 from station HLKY in Seoul, the headquarters of a network that soon connected the country's main urban centers. Religious programming was mixed with serious entertainment and high-quality news presentations. CBS also beamed programs to North Korea in the hope that the underground church there could draw some inspiration. CBS was soon followed by two other Christian broadcasting organizations. Although there is no Christian television station in Korea, important religious events such as Pope John Paul II's bicentennial mass are broadcast over commercial and government stations. And the Korea Video Evangelical Society provides religious videotapes for use in the VCRs that entertain passengers on intercity express buses.[18]

**Missionary training and sending.** Korean Protestants take pride in having a "sending church" with a missionary program of its own. They assert that this is one of the key distinctions between Korean Christianity and Christianity in other Asian countries, which have "receiving churches." They consider it a vital sign of a healthy and mature religious faith, something that keeps their church moving in creative directions.

Korea's overseas missionary program began before World War II with the sending of Presbyterian workers to Shandong province and the Jiandao area, in southern Manchuria, to work in Korean communities there. Even after the Korean War, while Korea itself lay in ruins, the largest churches managed to raise enough money to send a handful of Korean workers abroad. Today, Yŏngnak Church supports seven ordained missionaries in Guam, the Philippines, Indonesia, Taiwan, West Germany, Chile and Singapore, and eight lay workers in Pakistan, India, Nepal, Somalia and Malaysia. The Chung Hyŏn Presbyterian Church in Seoul has sent 17 missionary couples to a dozen countries over the years. Some of these work among overseas Koreans and some work in cooperation with the local churches to promote the evangelical message. A consortium of evangelical churches created the Korea Foreign Missions Association in 1972, an effort to generate a massive missionary program; they plan to train ten thousand missionaries by the year 2000—without Western help or influence. Neither is there any dearth of volunteers for missionary service: at the 1980 "Here's Life, Korea!" crusade, 300,000 young people reportedly offered to spend a year in overseas missionary service.[19]

Koreans have also started sharing their experiences with Christians in other countries by setting up training centers in Seoul. The Asian Center for Theological Studies (ACTS) is an institute that attracts seminarians and ministers from other countries to study the adaptation of Christianity to the local scene. The Third World Leadership Center at the Presbyterian Theological Seminary likewise invites students from around the world to study the growth of the Korean church and devise strategies for the evangelization of their home countries.

What do foreign students learn in these institutes? The premise is that the Korean church is a better model for churches in the developing world than the church in America or Europe. The adaptation of Christianity in Korea and the history of the church in times of adversity, pat-

[18]Jay Kwon Kim, "The Impact of Mass Communications," in Ro and Nelson, *op. cit.*, p. 155.
[19]Kim Chang-in, "A Church in Middle Class Suburbia: Secrets of Growth in the Chung Hyeon Presbyterian Church," in Ro and Nelson, *op. cit.*, p. 255; Park Cho-Choon, David J. Cho and Kim Joon Gon, in Ro and Nelson, op. cit., pp. 209, 113 and 35.

terns of leadership, organization, growth, finance, and outreach are all experiences that Koreans believe are worth teaching Christians from other countries. The fact that Korea itself has had a unique experience with Christianity in Asia does not detract from their determination to spread the gospel and, perhaps, the news of their own achievements.

**The Korean Catholic Church Today.**

The Catholic community in South Korea is estimated at over 1.6 million members in 633 parishes. There are 11 dioceses, and Seoul, Taegu, and Kwangju are archdioceses. There are 21 male and 42 female religious communities, and as of 1984 the church leadership numbered as follows:[20]

|          | Korean | Foreign | Total |
|----------|--------|---------|-------|
| Bishops  | 15     | 3       | 18    |
| Priests  | 1,000  | 227     | 1,227 |
| Brothers | n.a.   | n.a.    | 257   |
| Sisters  | 3,295  | 161     | 3,456 |

These statistics reflect substantial growth and devolution in the Catholic church since the eve of the Korean War, when Catholics numbered only 157,000. The war decimated the ranks of Korean priests, making the church once again dependent on foreign clergy for an additional period. Through the 1950s the leadership had a strong foreign component: the missionary orders carried the interest of the worldwide church to Korea and made critical contributions to the postwar relief effort and the reconstruction of church institutions. Foreign priests manned many pastorates, and foreign nuns directed many of the women's orders. Through the determined efforts of this combined Korean and foreign force, church membership grew from 160,000 in 1953 to 530,000 in just nine years. The succession of senior churchmen appointed by the Vatican as Apostolic Delegates concentrated on higher education and seminary training, so that in 1962, the year of the second Vatican Council, the Korean church was placed under its own hierarchy. Kim Su-hwan became the first Korean archbishop. In 1969 he was elected Cardinal, thus enabling Korean Catholics to have a role in deciding worldwide church policy.

Since establishment of the Korean Catholic hierarchy in 1962, the international effort has continued, but in a supporting role. The American Maryknoll mission counts Korea as its second oldest field (the first was South China) and the field with the longest continuous presence (not counting World War II). Though first active in the Pyongyang area, along with the Presbyterians, the Maryknolls were obliged to reorganize their work south of the 38th parallel after the war. When the Korean War broke out in 1950, Maryknoll missioners set up an emergency clinic

[20]*Korea Herald*, May 3, 1984, p. S-3; *Korea Times*, May 4, 1984, p. S-6.

34

in Pusan, which has become one of Korea's finest hospitals, run since 1970 by Korean sisters. Monsignor George Carroll, a Maryknoll representative, played a key role as organizer and administrator of the combined relief efforts of all the churches in Korea just after the war. Maryknoll missioners have continued working within the Korean hierarchy since 1962, often as lay workers volunteering for brief periods to lend their professional specialties to Catholic schools and training institutions. They have introduced such innovative programs as church-sponsored credit unions, which enable members to escape the ruinous interest rates in the money markets, health cooperatives in fishing villages, and teacher training programs for teachers of handicapped children. They have joined with Protestants in urban industrial evangelism, relating the Christian message to the special problems of factory workers and putting pressure on management to respect the rights of workers. In these ways the foreign missionary effort has evolved along with the changing needs of the Korean Catholic church, with fewer workers in positions of authority as formal missioners and more in positions where they serve as resource people and consultants, bringing in new ideas for adaptation to the Korean social scene.[21]

This social concern has put the Catholic church in a delicate political position on numerous occasions. Korean Catholics themselves have been in the front ranks of the political opposition, where they have made common cause with dissenting Christians of all denominations. Cardinal Kim Su-hwan, who is personally respected by Koreans in all walks of life for his reasonable attitudes, walks a tightrope between confrontation and collusion, counseling moderation but taking strong personal stands on human rights issues. This has given the Catholic church a high profile in modern Korean history and an influence far beyond its own membership.

**Major institutions and types of work.** The scope of Catholic work in Korea today is significant. There are 26 Catholic hospitals and 24 clinics and dispensaries in South Korea, and 25 leprosy centers. Catholic kindergartens and schools enroll 72,458 children and there are eight Catholic colleges and universities, of which the most distinguished are Sŏgang University and Catholic College, the main training ground for the priesthood. Other leading institutions are the Catholic Medical College, run by the Seoul archdiocese, Sacred Heart Sisters' College for Women, in Seoul, and Hyosŏng University for Women in Taegu, run by the Taegu archdiocese. Seminaries train priests in Seoul, Taegu, and Kwangju, and a fourth seminary is due to open in Suwon. In 1984 the number of seminarians-in-training was 751.

**The visit of Pope John Paul II.** Korean Catholics celebrated their bicentennial in May 1984. Pope John Paul II was on hand for the observ-

---

[21]"Korea, Land of Contradictions," special issue of *Maryknoll*, March 1982, *passim*.

ances, which were highlighted by a special mass in Yŏido Plaza during which the pontiff canonized 103 of the martyrs who died in the great persecutions of the nineteenth century. Certain papal gestures were especially appreciated. His plane flew in via the scheduled route of the Korean Airlines jet that had been shot down by Soviet fighters over Sakhalin the previous September. The Pope paid a courtesy call on President Chun Doo Hwan and met with community leaders at Sŏgang University. He also journeyed to Kwangju for an open-air "day of reconciliation" mass for common people, and to Sorok-do (Little Deer Island), to visit patients in the leper colony there. Korean Catholics spent the weekend sharing their history in a special spirit of unity and thanksgiving.

### Christianity as a Korean Religion.

No one observing the pope's visit and the celebrations of the Catholic bicentennial (or the Protestant centennial, which followed in the same year) could escape the impression that Christianity is now a Korean people's religion and no longer a foreign import. People often contrast the success of Christianity in Korea with the difficulties of the church in China and Japan, and end up looking for unique cultural characteristics that may account for Korea's greater receptivity to the Gospel. Such comparisons tend to denigrate Chinese and Japanese Christians, among whom there is, after all, considerable vitality. Yet there is no denying the special dynamism of the church in Korea, and the reasons for it are a topic of constant comment.

**Reasons for church growth.** Ro Bong Rin, a Korean missionary scholar who teaches in Taiwan at Tung-hai University, attributes Korean church growth to a number of circumstantial and spiritual factors. Japanese oppression of the Korean church from 1905 to 1945 cast it as a champion of Korean nationalism. The use of the native *Han'gŭl* alphabet by the church further asserted the solidarity of Christianity and nationalism under colonial rule. Church schools were the only modern alternative to education by the Japanese; hence attendance at mission schools carried with it a sense of boycotting the Japanese. Common people who had suffered discrimination because of the rigid stratification of Korean society enjoyed new social mobility in Christian organizations, which tried to be egalitarian. And the services, ceremonies and activities of the church provided important opportunities for self-expression and social contact.

As for spiritual reasons for church growth, Dr. Ro cites a spiritual hunger among Koreans arising from suffering through colonialism and civil war, the attractions of Christian ideas of salvation, the echoes in Christianity of other faiths such as Buddhism (heaven and hell) and shamanism (miracles, sacrifices and priesthood), and the fact that the use of *Han'gŭl* made scriptural study possible for large numbers of people. The church's stress on personal evangelism on a one-to-one basis has been especially effective in urban areas, where migration from the countryside has created large communities of strangers who miss their village neighborhoods and are desperately lonely in the city.[22]

Pak Cho-jun, a former pastor of Yŏngnak Church, also attributes the strength of the church to its heritage of suffering and its emphasis on personal evangelism, prayer and Bible study. He argues that the church faces the challenge of filling the spiritual void in Korea, which has been created by materialism and the obsession with economic development. He believes that today's church has replaced the Western missionaries as the catalyst for spiritual change in Korea and that Korea can offer the rest of the world an example of a non-Western national Christianity.[23]

The theme of Korean national Christianity is articulated by Harold Hong, former president of the Methodist Theological Seminary in Seoul. Like many Korean Christians he sees Korea as a "new Israel." "It would be unfair," he writes:

> to say that the Korean people were more receptive and responsive to the Christian gospel than any other nation in Asia. But we strongly believe that we are now the chosen people of God and that we are under the special providence of God. This strong faith has actually made the Korean church the most rapidly growing church in the world.[24]

Dr. Hong's sentiments represent those of many Korean Christians today and reflect the church's confidence in its purpose and historic role within Korean society.

---

[22]Ro Bong Rin, "Non-spiritual Factors in Church Growth," in Ro and Nelson, *op. cit.*, pp. 159–170.

[23]Park Cho-Choon, in Ro and Nelson, *op. cit.*, pp. 202–206.

[24]Harold S. Hong, "Social, Political and Psychological Aspects of Church Growth," in Ro and Nelson, *op. cit.*, p. 181.

# V. Church and State

The conservative Christian majority in Korea stresses spiritual questions and tends to avoid conflict over temporal issues. Indeed, given the uncertainties of daily life, the church's soothing spirituality is one of its attractions. In the political realm, the mainstream church "renders unto Caesar the things that are Caesar's" and heeds the Apostle Paul's advice in Romans 25:40: "He who resists the authorities resists what God has appointed."

Nevertheless, since its days as a center of the opposition to Japanese colonial rule, the Christian church has been involved in politics. Syngman Rhee, South Korea's first president from 1948 to 1960, was a prominent Methodist. His successor in 1960–61, Prime Minister Chang Myŏn, was a leading Catholic. Some people say that when Rhee was overthrown in 1960 following a corrupt election, and when Chang's ineptitude brought on a military coup in 1961, Christianity was discredited in the way the fall of the Yi dynasty discredited Confucianism in 1910 and the fall of Koryŏ discredited Buddhism in 1392. Korea's "modern" Christians were pushed aside by the more up-to-date military.

**The dissenting church.** Military rule, which began in 1961, did not offend Korean Christians; in fact, they approved of the new regime's efforts to bring about order and discipline. They also observed that the regime of Park Chung Hee officially espoused freedom of religion and continued the practice of staffing a chaplains' corps for the military services. Christians also benefited along with everyone else from the rapid economic growth that began after several years. However, General Park, after promising to restore Korea to civilian rule, retired from the army and ran for president himself. Later on, his supporters changed the constitution to permit him to run for reelection indefinitely. As opposition developed, he became more dictatorial, using national security as a pretext to limit the freedom of his critics, many of whom were in the church. In the last free presidential election in 1971, Park was challenged by Kim Dae Jung, a Catholic, who won 45.3 percent of the vote. The following year, when Park declared a state of emergency and began ruling by decree, Kim's supporters naturally were frustrated and joined the ranks of the emerging anti-Park coalition.

Much of the opposition to Park turned on human rights issues. There were several serious incidents. Park's secret police, the Korean Central Intelligence Agency (KCIA), kidnapped Kim Dae Jung while he was in Japan in 1973 and forcibly returned him to Korea for detention. There were roundups of alleged communists, who were convicted and sometimes executed on the basis of forced confessions. Public figures who spoke out against torture or for fundamental freedoms or who criticized Park's government were subjected to arrest and harassment.

Christians became involved in the opposition in various ways. Despite President Park's emergency decrees forbidding opposition or criticism, the church continued to serve as a gathering point for those willing to speak out for human rights, even at the risk of prison. A human rights campaign in 1974, for example, was led by a number of prominent Christians, many of whom soon went to prison themselves on various charges relating to "instigating rebellion." These included Pak Hyong-gyu and the brothers Mun Ik-hwan and Mun Tong-hwan, all Presbyterian ministers; Kim Chi-ha, the Catholic poet who specialized in satires about the regime and the materialism of modern Korean life; Yonsei University professors Kim Tong-gil (American history, specializing in Lincoln), and Kim Chan-guk (Theology); and Catholic Bishop Daniel Chi Hak-sun, who issued a personal "Declaration of Conscience" denouncing the Park dictatorship.

Christian organizations, as well as individuals, challenged Park's decrees in 1974. The National Christian Council, ostensibly representing 3.5 million Protestants, petitioned the president to rescind his more oppressive decrees (which he did, but only temporarily), and the Presbyterian General Assembly passed a resolution opposing the "nondemocratic dictatorship" and corruption (i.e., " . . . the bribing of officials is carried on in broad daylight before the eyes of the people").[25] Urban Industrial Mission, an interdenominational ministry to factory workers that was dedicated to helping bring about humane conditions in the workplace, was particularly hard-pressed by the government because it challenged the low-wage system upon which Park was basing Korea's economic growth.[26]

The church, particularly its dissident wing, maintained its active opposition to Park's excesses until his death in 1979. On March 1, 1976, for example, an ecumenical Independence Day mass at Seŏul's Myongdong Cathedral turned into an antigovernment meeting when a number of prominent civic and religious leaders issued a "Declaration for Democracy" and were promptly arrested. One of these was Kim Dae Jung, the Catholic politician who had challenged Park Chung Hee in the presidential election of 1971. The Myŏng-dong incident helped forge a potent alliance between Protestant and Catholic dissidents that has continued to the present.

### The Dissenting Church in the 1980s.

After Park Chung Hee was assassinated by the head of his own KCIA in October 1979, there was a period of several months during which,

[25]Emergency Christian Conference on Korean Problems, editors, *Documents on the Struggle for Democracy in Korea*, Tokyo: Shinkyo Shuppansha, 1975, p. 211.
[26]For Urban Industrial Mission see *Korea Calling* (Seoul), June 1962; November 1968; and December 1969; see also Peggy Billings, *Fire Beneath the Frost*, New York: Friendship Press, 1984, pp. 58–65.

despite martial law, many signs pointed to a relaxation and return to democratic rule. However, the army remained in control behind the scenes and a new strongman emerged as Park's successor. Major-General Chun Doo Hwan seized control of the army in a coup in December, appointed classmates from his military academy graduating class to the high command, and by the spring of 1980 was nearly in a position to take the presidency for himself.

The opposition coalition did not rest during this period. By late spring, Korea was suffering the consequences of the worldwide economic downturn, growth had come almost to a standstill, and there was rampant discontent. The situation deteriorated steadily as civilian authorities proved unable to deal with the rising economic and political demands of workers, students and opposition politicians. There were violent outbreaks. In Sabuk, striking mineworkers took over the town and caused considerable property damage before winning a wage increase. Students coordinated street demonstrations demanding faster democratization. These created a bandwagon effect among young people. Opposition politicians such as Kim Dae Jung, who had just been granted amnesty from his alleged crimes, took advantage of the opportunity to address large crowds—tens of thousands by mid-May—in which he denounced the military clique of Chun Doo Hwan. The military, for its part, recognized all this as having dangerous revolutionary potential.

**Christians in the Kwangju Incident of May 1980.** On May 17 the army cracked down, closing the universities, imposing total press censorship, and rounding up scores of leading intellectuals, religious leaders and opposition politicians, including Kim Dae Jung. Martial law, already in effect over most of the country, was extended everywhere.

It is still difficult to get the full story of what happened next in Kwangju, the capital of South Chŏlla Province in the heart of Kim Dae Jung's home district. What is known is that Kim's arrest set off massive demonstrations by students and citizens. Chun Doo Hwan's martial law command answered by sending in special forces, "Black Berets," who dealt at random with the demonstrators by using clubs and bayonets. Militant demonstrators then raided government weapons stocks and drove the Black Berets from the city. They held the city for five days, during which the government positioned a substantial regular army force for an invasion and mass rallies within the city were held to organize the resistance. Before –dawn on May 27 the army marched into the center of the city, inflicting casualties on those who were holding the provincial capital building. The government estimated the death toll during the entire uprising, from May 18 to May 27, at 191; the dissident community claims ten times that number, while press observers and

41

foreign residents of Kwangju estimate the total somewhere in between.[27]

There was little overt church involvement in the Kwangju uprising, though there were many Christians among the tens of thousands of citizens who joined the rebellion in the streets. The local Catholic community, centering on the Kwangju diocesan headquarters and seminary, was especially outraged at the treatment of Kim Dae Jung. Church organizations helped circulate information. The Christian Broadcasting Station became caught in a crossfire when it was taken over by martial law troops and then stormed by demonstrators. The staff of the Christian Hospital took in many of the dead and wounded. A student who led in the demonstrations was hidden for more than a year afterwards by a Catholic priest. Thus Christian institutions and individuals were caught up in the incident, even though the church as a body had little to do with how it began. And later, in the period of terror which followed Kwangju, during which all opposition leaders were in jail or otherwise silenced, the church as a body was noticeably quiet. The events of May 1980 were truly frightening, and together with fear over the concurrent economic slowdown, they made political opposition seem like a dangerous waste of energy.

Although most of the church remained politically quiet, the violent events of May 1980 drove a radical minority to bolder action. There were dramatic instances of self-sacrifice such as the suicide of Kim Ŭi-gi, a Methodist student who committed public suicide at the National Christian Council Building, and of Kim Chŏng-t'ae, an unemployed laborer who committed suicide in protest over the Kwangju incident in June 1980. Such events further served to drive a wedge between politically active Christians and those more willing to give in to the government. There was suspicion on both sides, the radicals accused of using the church for their own political purposes, and the conservative majority accused of collaborating with a military dictatorship. The tension within the church has continued to this day and it is not likely to diminish anytime soon.

The "dismissed professors". At the time of the Kwangju incident, the government forced the churches, universities and news media to

[27]Five years later, during a National Assembly investigation of the incident, the Kwangju vital statistics for May-June 1980 were found to show 2,627 deaths, as opposed to an average monthly death rate of 264 for the rest of the year. The Ministry of Home Affairs explained that the inflated figure was the result of a "clerical error," because the death rate column was next to the population increase column in the records, and the population increase was also shown at 2,627. *Korea Herald*, U.S. edition, June 9, 1985, p. 1. See the same issue for the defense minister's report of the Kwangju incident to the National Assembly in June 1985. For a relatively dispassionate account of the incident in the context of South Korean politics in 1979–80, see Robert Shaplen, "Letter from South Korea," *The New Yorker*, November 17, 1980, pp. 174–207. For the dissident community's version see Pacific-Asia Resources Center, *Korea, May 1980: People's Uprising in Kwangju*, Tokyo: Pacific-Asia Resources Center, 1980.

dismiss a group of 80 or more opinion leaders known to have opposed the rise of Chun Doo Hwan. Many were imprisoned and released on condition that they not return to their former jobs or speak about politics, though they were allowed to move around and work elsewhere if they could find employment. Eventually the emerging opposition of the 1980s rallied around this community of "dismissed professors." It was not an easy time for them personally or professionally; and yet a certain fond notoriety grew up around them as they coped with help from their friends. Professors preached; teachers wrote; reporters lectured; many traveled and studied abroad and broke new ground in research and writing. Overseas churches offered funds to support the dismissed clergymen. The American embassy, to its credit, displayed conspicuous interest in many of the professors, particularly the ones with American educations, inviting them to U.S. Information Agency seminars and to receptions at the ambassador's home. And when at length they were given back their rights in 1984, most found that their colleagues had kept their jobs open for them and were ready to welcome them back with warmth and respect.

**The dissenting church today.** By 1982, once the initial shock of Kwangju wore off, the dissident community grew bolder again. As before, clergymen were in the front rank. Ministers spoke out against human rights abuses. A dozen major leaders wrote a letter to President Chun protesting the use of torture in prison. In June a group of seven leading pastors issued a "Statement on Social Injustice" condemning inequities in the economic system, denouncing the way the Chun regime took power, and quoting Amos 5:24: "Let judgement run down as waters and righteousness as a mighty stream."[28]

The dissident community in the mid-1980s is linked with the church leadership and often uses church facilities. By 1983 the dissenting church was back in the public eye. For example, the National Christian Council sponsors an annual Human Rights Week, which culminates in an ecumenical service featuring leading figures in the movement. At the Human Rights Sunday service in Seoul's Anglican Cathedral in December 1983, the N.C.C. circulated its own "Declaration of Human Rights" along with a detailed report on students arrested during demonstrations over the course of the year. Memorial notices entitled "Who Killed Hwang Chŏng-ha?" circulated under the auspices of the Korea Student Christian Federation, the Korea Christian Youth Association, and the United Youth for Democratization, calling attention to the recent death of a demonstrator at Seoul National University. Other documents demanded freedom for the "dismissed professors" and an end to blacklisting, a greater effort for economic justice, including relief for

[28]Quoted in Henry Scott-Stokes, "Korea's Church Militant," *New York Times Magazine*, Nov. 28, 1982, p. 69.

workers from low wages and long hours, and exclusion of American nuclear weapons from Korea.

Under these circumstances the government naturally accused dissident Christians of abusing the right of religious freedom. Just after the 1983 Human Rights Week service, for example, the Minister of Culture and Information spoke of the "growing need for a positive, developmental change in the Christian world of Korea if the religion is to serve in its truest sense the people and the changing society. . . ."[29] This is a matter of definition, to be sure, for the dissident community *does* see itself "serving the people and changing society." The "dismissed professors," blacklisted ministers, and harassed Urban Industrial Mission workers, it seems safe to say, have been criticizing the regime out of a different vision of Korean society.

**Minjung Ideology: Toward a Korean Theology of Dissent.[30]**

Since the 1960s, dissenting elements within the church have been brewing a unique Korean theology which they call "*Minjung* theology." The word *minjung* means "masses," and Minjung theology is decidedly populist, even proletarian, in emphasis. Its association with the working class gives it a political ring, in contrast to the relatively apolitical ideology of mainstream Korean Christians. Minjung thinkers include young, articulate foreign-trained churchmen and scholars. They can communicate in English and have many international contacts, and so have generated considerable interest overseas. Mainstream Christians sometimes object that the Minjung theologians get a disproporionate share of international attention; and yet since they are prominent in the political opposition, it is likely that without worldwide attention they would surely suffer even more than is the case.

Minjung theology, which is reminiscent of liberation theology in Latin America, asserts the uniqueness of Korea. It holds that the history of the Korean people is a history of oppression, of sadness and frustration which has given rise to a unique mind-set called *han*. *Han* is a pent-up anger mixed with depression over situations that cannot be changed: the unfairness and injustice of life; the disappointments and disillusionments of history and politics.

Korean Christians share the feeling of *han*, but their faith moves them to action, even when there is no human hope for change or improvement. Indeed, Minjung Christians feel a duty to challenge the odds for

[29]*Korea Times*, Dec. 17, 1983, quoted in G. Cameron Hurst, "Christianity in Korea," *USFI Reports*, 1983, no.26 (Asia), p. 8.
[30]For an explanation of Minjung theology see David Kwang-sun Suh, *Theology, Ideology and Culture*, Hong Kong: World Christian Student Federation, 1983, and Tong Hwan (Stephen Moon), "Korean Minjung Theology: An Introduction," in Wonmo Dong editor, *Korean-American Relations at Crossroads*, Princeton, N.J.: The Association of Korean Christian Scholars in North America, 1982, pp. 12–34.

the sake of ordinary people and to protest injustice and oppression no matter how powerful. It is a romantic ideology, an interesting mixture of pessimism and optimism.

Many Minjung leaders were among those dismissed from their jobs in 1980 and recently reinstated. The government sees a clear connection among Minjung theology, student activism, labor unrest and overseas criticism of the Seoul regime. Urban Industrial Mission, the interfaith ministry to factory workers, for example, is the quintessence of Minjung activism. Minjung activism is gaining special popularity among university students, who freely mix political and religious symbols in their messages. Student rallies often feature quasi-religious folk dancing and ceremonies from Korea's shamanist tradition. These are meant to recall the *han*, or suffering, of the common people under oppressive regimes of the past and, therefore, are of a piece with Minjung theology. Even on Christian college campuses one sees mock ceremonies and sacrifices that are based on shamanist practice. The early Protestant missionaries in Korea would have recoiled in horror from such idolatrous practices in their schools. But in the context of Minjung theology they fit because they refer to the sin of oppression throughout Korean history.

Minjung theology is new, but there have already been many attempts to make it intelligible to foreign readers. One key point is that it is non-Marxist and does not use Marxist language. This, of course, is a requirement in South Korea. But because it stresses unique Korean roots and emphasizes its relationship to contemporary life in South Korea, it has avoided the taint of communism that the government, no doubt, would like to attach to it.

# VI. Christianity and American-Korean Relations

The American commitment to South Korea is embodied in the mutual security treaty of 1954 and in a web of moral commitments arising from the years of contact, the investment of lives and money, and the American role in South Korea's development as a democratic/capitalist model for the Third World. At present, more than 2,000 American civilians live in Seoul and there are more in the provinces. Nearly 40,000 U.S. military men and women are stationed in Korea. Americans from many walks of life have died in Korea, including 33,629 military personnel in the Korean War. Many American-educated Koreans occupy top positions in government, education and business. The Korean community in the United States is nearing a million. All these are substantial links between the people of Korea and the United States.

There is a considerable reservoir of good will in Korea toward the United States. South Koreans—including millions of refugees from the North—genuinely appreciate America's contributions to their freedom from communist rule. There is also a considerable good feeling about nonmilitary support: the role of missionary work, particularly in modern education, and private and public economic assistance. Americans rarely feel unsafe or threatened in Korea and are often the recipients of kindness simply because they *are* Americans. "Gratitude" would not be too strong a word to describe the feelings expressed formally and informally toward Americans on many occasions. And yet it is understandable that, after so many years of having to be "grateful" in an unequal relationship, Koreans are now much more discriminating about the kinds of help and influence they are willing to accept from the United States.

The American-Korean relationship is clearly changing. Korea is now a security and trading partner and much less of a client. Exports are rising, the cities are booming, the 1988 Summer Olympics are to be held in Seoul, and there is a new self-respect in Korea that demands an end to the old unequal relationship with the United States. Both sides are having to adjust. It sometimes seems hard for Americans, given the long unequal relationship, to think of Korea as a partner or to work effectively with Koreans as colleagues in Korean-controlled organizations. It also seems difficult for Koreans to stop expecting Americans to give them special treatment. Yet the future requires that both sides change their attitudes, and that the Koreans accept the responsibilities that come with their success.

## American-Korean Relations and the Church.
One area where the American-Korean relationship already has

passed into a more equal phase is in the church. In 1984 the bicentennial of Catholicism and the centennial of Protestantism offered many occasions to see that the Korean church is entirely free of foreign control. Korean church leaders gave full credit to the missionaries for their contributions. The Presbyterian General Assembly invited many retired missionaries back to Seoul at church expense to be honored at the anniversary celebration in September. But in 1984 there were no missionaries in positions of policymaking or control. Most of those remaining were in specific institutions in staff, faculty and liaison positions.

**The dissident critique of the missionary effort.**[31] One type of stock-taking that has been going on in the Korean church is a critical reassessment of the missionary effort, coming mainly, as might be expected, from the dissident/activist wing of the church. This critique of missionary motives and tactics is related to rising nationalism and an emerging critique of American-Korean relations in general. For example, a frequent charge is that the missionaries transplanted American denominationalism to Korea and thereby divided the Protestant church at the outset. This is one reason, it is said, for the Korean church's tendency to splinter.

Another criticism is the anti-intellectualism of many early missionaries who opposed sending Korean converts abroad for higher education. They seemed to prefer to keep their protégés in Korea under their own influence, safe from liberal theology and the corruptions of modern life. This is one reason, it is said, for the pietistic, other-worldly orientation of the mainstream Korean Protestant church.

Still other criticisms relate to the ordeal of the Shintō shrine controversy in the 1930s, when some American missionaries counseled resistance (and thereby got their Korean converts in trouble with the Japanese) and other missionaries tried to be neutral (and later were accused of advising their Korean converts to collaborate). In an age of nationalism, missionaries make easy targets. The historical record offers ample evidence of their paternalistic attitudes and their other-worldly spiritualism mixed with unconcern for some of the realities of life in Korea at the time. The record is mixed, as is the record of the entire American relationship with Korea. There are many Koreans—both Christian and non-Christian—who would be quick to add that the results have been mostly for the good.

Most Korean Christians support their government's alliance with the United States and are satisfied with American assurances of protection in case of war. Others are concerned about the way American culture overwhelms Korea in some respects, devaluing tradition. Still others

[31]Much of this critique is summarized in David Kwang-sun Suh, "American Missionaries and a Hundred Years of Korean Protestantism" (unpublished paper, 1982).

decry the militarization of their country, the endless tension caused by the confrontation with North Korea, and the tendency toward military rule. They charge that America's preoccupation with the Cold War means automatic American support for any anti-communist regime in Seoul no matter how dictatorial. University students, following world-wide movements, express concern at how the American alliance has involved Korea in the dangers of the nuclear arms race and how the presence of American nuclear weapons in Korea makes their country a target for the Soviet Union's recently-deployed SS-20 missiles in Siberia. They also like to emphasize the economic imbalances between the United States and Korea, and the contrived dependence of the Korean economy on American consumers.

Because of their numbers, organization and education, Korean Christians will always have a powerful influence on the course of U.S.-Korean relations. The dissident community within the church is especially significant because of its leavening potential. At present the church in general seems contented with overall trends in Korea, including political liberalization. It does not seem likely to develop into an organized political force in the immediate future, though it would be formidable if events were to politicize the mainstream; but Korean Christians as a group and as individuals will certainly continue to play leading roles in Korea's development as a modern state.

# VII. Conclusion

The success of Christianity in South Korea has been influenced by history, politics, and the unique characteristics of the Korean people. Some commentators ascribe it in part to Korea's shamanist tradition. Others attribute it to the spiritual climate created by the suffering of the Korean people under oppressive rulers. Most Christians themselves attribute it to the grace of God, and many concur with Dr. Harold Hong's proposition that Korea is a special place with a special part to play in the history of the world church. Whatever interpretation one chooses, it is nonetheless remarkable that Christianity, which began as an alien creed, has such a powerful influence in Korea today. One cannot explain it as the success of foreign propagandists, nor merely as the phenomenon of "rice Christians" embracing the missionaries' religion in order to get food or medicine or even modern education. Since the Korean War, all these things have been more readily available from other sources, yet it is in the postwar period that the Korean church has experienced its most explosive growth. Today's church is a Koreanized church, with theological and organizational undertones that echo Korean tradition. The ancient shamanist strain is there. So are Confucian ideals of harmony, reciprocity, hierarchy and authority. So, too, is the neo-Confucianist tendency to split hairs over doctrine and to condemn deviations, a tendency manifested in political purges during the Yi dynasty. The foreign observer who expects the Korean church to look or act like the church back home will be surprised—and perhaps disillusioned. It must be taken on its own terms.

Although Christianity is now a Korean religion, it owes much to the foreign missionaries who first imported Christian ideas and institutions and who established, without doubt, the most significant people-to-people link ever to exist between Korea and the rest of the world. In the beginning this link was a conduit for modern ideas, for new and better ways of doing things, in addition to new and alien beliefs. Missionaries taught leadership to common people, fostering democratic ideas so they could run their own churches. They accepted the children of common people into their schools and taught them the entire modern curriculum of science, mathematics and world history—along with the Bible. They trained Korean doctors and nurses and deployed them in hospitals and clinics throughout the country to fight disease and malnutrition. Christianity today is only one of many modern and international influences on Korea, but earlier in this century it was very important as an alternative to the other great force for change—Japan. As such, Christianity gathered strength and support from Koreans who used church institutions as havens from Japanese oppression.

Much of the early growth of the church and the popularity of its institutions should be understood in light of the fact that Christianity enabled Korean believers to feel both patriotic and modern at the same time. When Japan ruled Korea, conditions combined to neutralize the contradictions between nationalism and Christianity that existed at the same time in China, and appear now to exist in North Korea. One might have expected many Koreans to have rejected Christianity after the end of the war in 1945, and many did. But the ordeal of national division and war after 1945 created a passionate anti-communism which lacked an organized ideological basis. Anti-communism, which might be called the state creed of South Korea, is no substitute for the spiritual void left by the destruction of so much tradition in so short a time. Ironically perhaps, it is Christianity, now translated into Korean Christianity, which fills that void for many South Koreans.

# Suggested Reading

Billings, Peggy. *Fire Beneath the Frost: The Struggles of the Korean People and Church*. New York: Friendship Press, 1984.

Blair, William Newton. *Gold in Korea*. New York: Presbyterian Church in the U.S.A., 1957.

Boettcher, Robert. *Gifts of Deceit: Sun Myung Moon, Tongsun Park, and the Korean Scandal*. New York: Holt, Rinehart and Winston, 1980.

Brown, G. Thompson. *Not by Might: A Century of Presbyterians in Korea*. Atlanta: Presbyterian Church in the U.S.A., 1984.

Buss, Claude A. *The United States and the Republic of Korea*. Stanford, Calif.: Hoover Institution Press, 1982.

Clark, Allen D. *A History of the Church in Korea*. Seoul: Christian Literature Society, 1971.

Clark, Charles Allen. *The Korean Church and the Nevius Methods*. Seoul: Christian Literature Society, 1937.

Cumings, Bruce, editor. *Child of Conflict: The Korean-American Relationship, 1943–1953*. Seattle and London: University of Washington Press, 1983.

Dong, Wonmo, editor. *Korean-American Relations at Crossroads*. Princeton, N.J.: The Association of Korean Christian Scholars in North America, 1982.

Emergency Christian Conference on Korean Problems. *Documents on the Struggle for Democracy in Korea*. Tokyo: Shinkyo Shuppansha, 1975.

Fisher, J. Ernest. *Democracy and Mission Education in Korea*. Seoul: Yonsei University Press, 1970.

Henderson, Gregory. *Korea: The Politics of the Vortex*. Cambridge, Mass.: Harvard University Press, 1968.

Hunt, Everett N., Jr. *Protestant Pioneers in Korea*. Maryknoll, N.Y.: Orbis Books, 1980.

Huntley, Martha. *Caring, Growing, Changing: A History of the Protestant Mission in Korea*. New York: Friendship Press, 1984.

Kim, Joseph Chang-mun, and Chung, John Jae-sun, editors. *Catholic Korea Yesterday and Today*. Seoul: Catholic Press, 1964.

*Korea Journal*. Special Issue entitled "200 Years of Korean Catholicism." August 1984.

Ku, Dae-yeol. *Korea under Colonialism: The March First Movement and Anglo-Japanese Relations*. Seoul: Royal Asiatic Society, Korea Branch, 1985.

Lee, Kibaik. *A New History of Korea*. translated by Edward W. Wagner with Edward J. Shultz. Cambridge, Mass.: Harvard University Press, 1985.

Lee, Kun Sam. *The Christian Confrontation with Shinto Nationalism*.

Philadelphia: The Presbyterian and Reformed Publishing Co., 1966.

Moffett, Samuel Hugh. *The Christians of Korea*. New York: Friendship Press, 1962.

Ogle, George E. *Liberty to the Captives*. Atlanta: John Knox Press, 1977.

Pacific-Asia Resources Center. *Korea May 1980: People's Uprising in Kwangju*. Tokyo: Pacific Asia Resources Center, 1980.

Paik, L. George. *The History of Protestant Missions in Korea, 1832–1910*. Seoul: Yonsei University Press, 1971.

Palmer, Spencer J. *Korea and Christianity*. Seoul: Royal Asiatic Society-/Hollym, 1967.

Rees, David. *Korea: The Limited War*. Baltimore, Md.: Penguin Books, 1964.

Ro, Bong-Rin and Nelson, Marlin L., editors. *Korean Church Growth Explosion*. Seoul: Word of Life Press, 1983.

Scott-Stokes, Henry. "Korea's Church Militant," *The New York Times Magazine*, Nov. 28, 1982.

Shaplen, Robert. "Letter from South Korea," *The New Yorker*. Nov. 17, 1980.

Shearer, Roy E. *Wildfire: Church Growth in Korea*. Grand Rapids, Mich.: Eerdmans Publishers, 1966.

Suh, David Kwang-sun. *Theology, Ideology and Culture*. Hong Kong: World Student Christian Federation, 1983.

U.S. House of Representatives. Committee on Foreign Affairs. Subcommittees on Asian and Pacific Affairs and on International Organizations and Movements. *Hearings on Human Rights in South Korea: Implications for U.S. Policy*. 93d Cong., 2d Sess., 1974.

U.S. House of Representatives. Committee on International Relations. Subcommittee on International Organizations. *Report on an Investigation of Korean-American Relations*. Committee Print, 95th Cong., 2d Sess., Oct. 31, 1978.

Yim, Kwan Ha. "Why South Korea's Dissidents Failed," *Asia*. March/April 1981.

# ABOUT THE AUTHOR

DONALD N. CLARK is Associate Professor of History at Trinity University in San Antonio. He earned his Ph.D. in East Asian history at Harvard University in 1978. His lifelong interest in Korea began with childhood, as the son of missionaries in Seoul. He has since lived in Korea as a Peace Corps Volunteer, Social Science Research Council Fellow, and Fulbright Scholar. He spent his Fulbright year at Yonsei University preparing a book on the history of the university.

Professor Clark is former Chairman of the Committee on Korean Studies of the Association for Asian Studies and a former councillor of the Korea Branch of the Royal Asiatic Society. He has published articles in various Korean studies journals and has contributed a chapter on Ming-Korean relations to the *Cambridge History of China*.

275.195
C592

74252

DATE DUE

DEC 14 '87

DEMCO 38-297